Knowing the Holy Spirit

—

Ten Classic Sermons on Prayer

Charles Haddon Spurgeon

Knowing the Holy Spirit

© 2019 by Cross-Points Books

All Scripture is taken from the *King James Version*.

Material sourced from The Metropolitan Tabernacle Pulpit Sermons

CONTENTS

Series Introduction

Foreword by Clay Kraby

1	Pentecostal Wind and Fire	1
2	The Sealing of the Spirit	21
3	The Spirit of Bondage and Adoption	40
4	The Power of the Holy Ghost	56
5	The Comforter	74
6	The Superlative Excellence of the Holy Spirit	90
7	The Holy Spirit's Threefold Conviction of Men	110
8	The Holy Ghost — The Great Teacher	130
9	The Holy Spirit's Chief Office	149
10	The Necessity of the Spirit's Work	165

Appendix: A Prayer to Live Worthy of the Gospel

About the Author

Ministries We Love

SERIES INTRODUCTION

The Rich Theology Made Accessible Series seeks to bolster the faith of busy Christians by making rich theology from time past more accessible.

Current Titles:
- Volume 1: *The Chief Exercise of Faith: John Calvin on Prayer*
- Volume 2: *Gospel Hope for Anxious Hearts: Trading Fear and Worry for the Peace of God* by Charles Spurgeon
- Volume 3: *Encouraged to Pray: Classic Sermons on Prayer* by Charles Spurgeon
- *Volume 4: Lessons from the Apostle Paul's Prayers* by Charles Spurgeon
- *Volume 5: Our Savior's Cries from the Cross* by Charles Spurgeon

Visit Cross-Points.org/richtheology to learn more or to explore additional titles.

JOIN THE CONVERSATION

Share your thoughts and favorite quotes on social media using the hashtag #KnowingtheHolySpirit or by mentioning us on social media:
- Twitter: @Cross_Points
- Facebook: @CrossPoints.Resources

FOREWORD

Those who are familiar with the life and ministry of C.H. Spurgeon have likely heard the anecdote that he would ascend to his pulpit saying quietly to himself at each step, "I believe in the Holy Spirit. I believe in the Holy Spirit." So great was the task at hand, the Prince of Preachers recognized that apart from the Spirit's work in and through him, he could do nothing.

Spurgeon's reliance on the work of the Spirit was not reserved for the moments before he addressed his congregation of several thousand on a Sunday morning. His entire life was marked by a conscious dependence on the Spirit, and we can say without hesitation that this dependence was a hallmark of Spurgeon's success in ministry.

This truth was not lost on Spurgeon, who stated that, "Without the Spirit of God we can do nothing. We are as ships without wind or chariots without steeds. Like branches without sap, we are withered. Like coals without fire, we are useless. As an offering without the sacrificial flame, we are unaccepted."

It is because of the Spirit's work through Spurgeon that he was able to reach untold thousands with his preaching, teaching, and writing. While there are none alive today who had the privilege of hearing Spurgeon preach, there are many who have nevertheless been ministered to by him through the many volumes of sermons and nearly 150 books he left behind.

I am one of those who count this Victorian-era preacher as having had a tremendous impact on my own life and ministry. His singular focus on the Gospel of Christ, his ability to present deep theological truths in easy-to-understand terms, and his affection for those he ministered to have been strong examples for me personally. Although I am far removed both in time and geography from Spurgeon's Metropolitan Tabernacle, there are few areas of ministry where his written works do not continue to provide helpful and relevant guidance.

Charles Spurgeon's ministry was so impactful because he sought first and foremost to make much of Jesus Christ through the enabling power of the Holy Spirit. He wrote, "We, my brethren, who are preachers of the Word, have but a short time to live; let us dedicate all that time to the glorious work of magnifying Christ." How can someone accomplish such a task? He continues, "If we alone had the task of glorifying Christ, we might be beaten; but as the Holy Spirit is the Glorifier of Christ, His glory is in very safe hands."

Every Christian is to be about the same business as Spurgeon was, seeking to magnify Christ and minister to others in a way that relies on the Spirit of God to operate in the souls of men. This is why Spurgeon has proven himself to be so worthy a guide towards a deeper understanding of the work and person of the Holy Spirit. He not only accomplished great things for the Kingdom of God, but he humbly recognized that any work of his hands – no matter how remarkable – would have been meaningless were it not for the Spirit's work in and through him.

In our day a biblical understanding of the Spirit's work is sorely needed. Confusion about who He is and what He does abounds, and too often we proceed through life relying on our power rather than His. Many contemporary works about the Holy Spirit are focused solely on either promoting or refuting the excesses of the extreme charismatic movement, and so there is a need to examine what Scripture has to say on the subject from a different vantage point. Spurgeon's sermons provide just such a vantage point. They are at once timeless expositions of the truth of God's Word and timely exhortations for the church to give proper, biblical focus on the person of the Holy Spirit.

As you read these selected sermons from Spurgeon, may you gain a greater understanding of and appreciation for the Spirit's work in your own life and ministry. We rejoice to know that it is He who convinces you of sin and gives power to your prayers of repentance; it is He who illuminates Scripture to your mind and enables you to glorify Christ with the work of your hands.

May each us go about our lives with a conscious and joyous dependence on the Spirit's work, saying with each step, "I believe in the Holy Spirit…I believe in the Holy Spirit…I believe in the Holy Spirit."

Clay Kraby is a pastor at Grace Baptist Church in Grand Forks, North Dakota and runs ReasonableTheology.org, a website dedicated to providing sound doctrine in plain language.

1
THE PENTECOSTAL WIND AND FIRE

"And suddenly there came a sound from heaven as of a rushing mighty wind, and it filled all the house where they were sitting. And there appeared unto them cloven tongues like as of fire, and it sat upon each of them. And they were all filled with the Holy Ghost, and began to speak with other tongues, as the Spirit gave them utterance."—*Acts 2:2–4*.

~

FROM the descent of the Holy Ghost at the beginning we may learn something concerning his operations at the present time. Remember at the outset that whatever the Holy Spirit was at the first that he is now, for as God he remaineth for ever the same: whatsoever he then did he is able to do still, for his power is by no means diminished. As saith the prophet Micah, "O thou that art named the house of Jacob, is the spirit of the Lord straitened?" We should greatly grieve the Holy Spirit if we supposed that his might was less to-day than in the beginning. Although we may not expect, and need not desire, the miracles which came with the gift of the Holy Spirit, so far as they were physical, yet we may both desire and expect that which was intended and symbolized by them, and we may reckon to see the like spiritual wonders performed among us at this day.

Pentecost, according to the belief of the Jews, was the time of the giving of the law; and if when the law was given there was a marvellous display of power on Sinai, it was to be expected that when the gospel was given, whose ministration is far more glorious, there should be some special unveiling of the divine presence. If at the commencement of the gospel we behold the Holy Spirit working great signs and wonders may we not expect a continuance—nay, if anything, an increased display—of his power as the ages roll on? The law vanished away, but the gospel will never vanish; it shineth more and more to the perfect millennial day; therefore, I reckon that, with the sole exception of physical miracles, whatever was wrought by the Holy Ghost at the first we may look to be wrought continually while the dispensation lasts. It ought not to be forgotten that Pentecost was the feast of first fruits; it was the time when the first ears of ripe corn were offered unto God. If, then, at the commencement of the gospel harvest we see so plainly the power of the Holy Spirit, may we not most properly expect infinitely more as the harvest advances, and most of all when the most numerous sheaves shall be ingathered? May we not conclude that if the Pentecost was thus marvellous the actual harvest will be more wonderful still?

This morning my object is not to talk of the descent of the Holy Spirit as a piece of history, but to view it as a fact bearing upon us at this hour, even upon us who are called in these latter days to bear our testimony for the truth. The Father hath sent us the Comforter that he may dwell in us till the coming of the Lord. The Holy Ghost has never returned, for he came in accordance with the Saviour's prayer, to abide with us for ever. The gift of the Comforter was not temporary, and the display of his power was not to be once seen and no more. The Holy Ghost is here, and we ought to expect his divine working among us: and if he does not so work we should search ourselves to see what it is that hindereth, and whether there may not be somewhat in ourselves which vexes him, so that he restrains his sacred energy, and doth not work among us as he did aforetime. May God grant that the meditation of this morning may increase our faith in the Holy Ghost, and inflame our desires towards him, so that we may look to see him fulfilling his mission among men as at the beginning.

I. First, I shall call your attention to THE INSTRUCTIVE SYMBOLS of the Holy Spirit, which were made prominent at Pentecost. They were two. There was a sound as of a rushing mighty wind, and there were cloven tongues as it were of fire.

Take the symbols separately. The first is *wind*—an emblem of Deity, and therefore a proper symbol of the Holy Spirit. Often under the Old Testament God revealed himself under the emblem of breath or wind: indeed, as most of you know, the Hebrew word for "wind" and "spirit" is the same. So, with the Greek word, when Christ talked to Nicodemus, it is not very easy for translators to tell us when he said "spirit" and when he said "wind;" indeed, some most correctly render the original all the way through by the word "wind," while others with much reason have also used the word "spirit" in their translation. The original word signified either the one or the other, or both. Wind is, of all material things, one of the most spiritual in appearance; it is invisible, ethereal, mysterious; hence, men have fixed upon it as being nearest akin to spirit. In Ezekiel's famous vision, when he saw the valley full of dry bones, we all know that the Spirit of God was intended by that vivifying wind which came when the prophet prophesied and blew upon the withered relics till they were quickened into life. "The Lord hath his way in the whirlwind," thus he displays himself when he works: "The Lord answered Job out of the whirlwind," thus he reveals himself when he teaches his servants.

Observe that this wind was on the day of Pentecost accompanied with a sound—a sound as of a rushing mighty wind; for albeit the Spirit of God can work in silence, yet in saving operations he frequently uses sound. I would be the last to depreciate meetings in which there is nothing but holy silence, for I could wish that we had more reverence for silence, and <u>it is in stillness that the inner life is nourished</u>; yet the Holy Ghost does not work for the advancement of the kingdom of God by silence alone, for faith cometh by hearing. There is a sound as of a rushing, mighty wind, when the word is sounded forth throughout whole nations by the publishing of the gospel. If the Lord had not given men ears or tongues silent worship would have been not only appropriate but necessary; but inasmuch as we have ears the Lord must have intended us to hear something, and as we have tongues he must have meant us to speak. Some of us would be glad to be quiet, but where the gospel has free course, there is sure to be a measure of noise and stir. The sound came on this occasion, no doubt, to call the attention of the assembly to what was about to occur, to arouse them, and to fill them with awe! There is something indescribably solemn about the rush of a rising tempest; it bows the soul before the sublime mystery of divine power. What more fitting as an attendant upon divine working than the deeply solemn rush of a mighty wind.

With this awe-inspiring sound as of a mighty wind, there was clear indication of its coming from heaven. Ordinary winds blow from this or that quarter of the skies, but this descended from heaven itself: it was distinctly like a down-draught from above. This sets forth the fact that the true Spirit, the Spirit of God, neither comes from this place nor that, neither can his power be controlled or directed by human authority, but his working is ever from above, from God himself. The work of the Holy Spirit is, so to speak, the breath of God, and his power is evermore in a special sense the immediate power of God. Coming downward, therefore, this mysterious wind passed into the chamber where the disciples were assembled, and filled the room. An ordinary rushing mighty wind would have been felt outside the room, and would probably have destroyed the house or injured the inmates, if it had been aimed at any one building; but this heavenly gust filled but did not destroy the room, it blessed but did not overthrow the waiting company.

The meaning of the symbol is that as breath, air, wind, is the very life of man, so is the Spirit of God the life of the spiritual man. By him are we quickened at the first; by him are we kept alive afterwards; by him is the inner life nurtured, and increased, and perfected. The breath of the nostrils of the man of God is the Spirit of God.

This holy breath was not only intended to quicken them, but to invigorate them. What a blessing would a breeze be just now to us who sit in this heavy atmosphere! How gladly would we hail a gust from the breezy down, or a gale from the open sea! If the winds of earth are so refreshing what must a wind from heaven be! That rushing mighty wind soon cleared away all earth-engendered damps and vapours; it aroused the disciples and left them braced up for the further work of the Lord. They took in great draughts of heavenly life; they felt animated, aroused, and bestirred. A sacred enthusiasm came upon them, because they were filled with the Holy Ghost; and, girt with that strength, they rose into a nobler form of life than they had known before.

No doubt this wind was intended to show the irresistible power of the Holy Ghost; for simple as the air is, and mobile and apparently feeble, yet set it in motion, and you feel that a thing of life is among you; make that motion more rapid, and who knows the power of the restless giant who has been awakened. See, it becomes a storm, a tempest, a hurricane, a tornado, a cyclone. Nothing can be more potent than the wind when it is thoroughly roused, and so, though the Spirit of God be despised among men, so much so that they do not even believe in his existence, yet let him work with the fulness of his power, and you will see what he can do. He comes softly, breathing like a gentle zephyr, which fans the flowers, but does not dislodge the insect of most gauzy wing, and our hearts are comforted. He comes like a stirring breeze, and we are quickened to a livelier diligence: our sails are hoisted and we fly before the gale. He comes with yet greater strength, and we prostrate ourselves in the dust as we hear the thunder of his power, bringing down with a crash false confidences and refuges of lies! How the firm reliances of carnal men, which seemed to stand like rocks, are utterly cast down! How men's hopes, which appeared to be rooted like oaks, are torn up by the roots before the breath of the convincing Spirit! What can stand against him? Oh! that we did but see in these latter days something of that mighty rushing wind which breaketh the cedars of Lebanon, and sweeps before it all things that would resist its power.

The second Pentecostal symbol was *fire*. Fire, again, is a frequent symbol of Deity. Abraham saw a burning lamp, and Moses beheld a burning bush. When Solomon had built his holy and beautiful house, its consecration lay in the fire of God descending upon the sacrifice to mark that the Lord was there; for when the Lord had dwelt aforetime in the tabernacle, which was superseded by the temple, he revealed himself in a pillar of cloud by day and a pillar of fire by night. "Our God is a consuming fire." Hence the symbol of fire is a fit emblem of God the Holy Spirit. Let us adore and worship him. Tongues of flame sitting on each man's head betoken a personal visitation to the mind and heart of each one of the chosen company. Not to consume them came the fires, for no one was injured by the flaming tongue; to men whom the Lord has prepared for his approach there is no danger in his visitations. They see God, and their lives are preserved; they feel his fires, and are not consumed. This is the privilege of those alone who have been prepared and purified for such fellowship with God.

The intention of the symbol was to show them that the Holy Spirit would illuminate them, as fire gives light. "He shall lead you into all truth." Henceforth they were to be no more children untrained, but to be teachers in Israel, instructors of the nations whom they were to disciple unto Christ: hence the Spirit of light was upon them. But fire doth more than give light: it inflames; and the flames which sat upon each showed them that they were to be ablaze with love, intense with zeal, burning with self-sacrifice; and that they were to go forth among men to speak not with the chill tongue of deliberate logic, but with burning tongues of passionate pleading; persuading and entreating men to come unto Christ that they might live. The fire signified in spiration. God was about to make them speak under a divine influence, to speak as the Spirit of God should give them utterance. Oh! blessed symbol, would God that all of us experienced its meaning to the full and that the tongue of fire did sit upon every servant of the Lord. May a fire burn steadily within to destroy our sin, a holy sacrificial flame to make us whole burnt offerings unto God, a never-dying flame of zeal for God, and devotion to the cross.

Note that the emblem was not only fire, but a tongue of fire; for God meant to have a speaking church: not a church that would fight with the sword—with that weapon we have nought to do—but a church that should have a sword proceeding out of its mouth, whose one weapon should be the proclamation of the gospel of Jesus Christ. I should think from what I know of some preachers that when they had their Pentecost the influence sat upon them in the form of tongues of flowers; but the apostolic Pentecost knew not flowers, but flames. What fine preaching we have nowadays! What new thoughts, and poetical turns! This is not the style of the Holy Ghost. Soft and gentle is the flow of smooth speech which tells of the dignity of man, the grandeur of the century, the toning down of all punishment for sin, and the probable restoration of all lost spirits, including the arch-fiend himself. This is the Satanic ministry, subtle as the serpent, bland as his seducing words to Eve. The Holy Ghost calls us not to this mode of speech. Fire, intensity, zeal, passion as much as you will, but as for aiming at effect by polished phrases and brilliant periods—these are fitter for those who would deceive men than for those who would tell them the message of the Most High. The style of the Holy Ghost is one which conveys the truth to the mind in the most forcible manner,—it is plain but flaming, simple but consuming. The Holy Spirit has never written a cold period throughout the whole Bible, and never did he speak by a man a lifeless word, but evermore he gives and blesses the tongue of fire.

These, then, are the two symbols; and I should like you carefully to observe how the Holy Spirit teaches us by them. When he came from the Father to his Son Jesus it was as a dove. Let peace rest on that dear sufferer's soul through all his days of labour and through the passion which would close them. His anointing is that of peace: he needed no tongue of flame, for he was already all on fire with love. When the Holy Spirit was bestowed by the Son of God upon his disciples it was as breath—"He breathed on them and said, Receive the Holy Ghost." To have life more abundantly is a chief necessity of servants of the Lord Jesus, and therefore thus the Holy Ghost visits us. Now that we have the Holy Spirit from Christ as our inner life and quickening he also comes upon us with the intent to use us in blessing others, and this is the manner of his visitation,—he comes as the wind, which wafts the words we speak, and as fire which burns a way for the truth we utter. Our words are now full of life and flame; they are borne by the breath of the Spirit, and they fall like fire-flakes, and set the souls of men blazing with desire after

[Margin note: "Half the truth is Hell"]

God. If the Holy Spirit shall rest upon me or upon you, or upon any of us, to qualify us for service, it shall be after this fashion—not merely of life for ourselves, but of fiery energy in dealing with others. Come on us even now, O rushing mighty wind and tongue of fire, for the world hath great need. It lies stagnant in the malaria of sin and needs a healing wind; it is shrouded in dreadful night, and needs the flaming torch of truth. There is neither health nor light for it but from thee, O blessed Spirit; come, then, upon it through thy people.

Now put these two symbols together; only mind what you are at. Wind and fire together! I have kept them separate in my discourse hitherto; and you have seen power in each one; what are they together? Rushing mighty wind alone how terrible! Who shall stand against it? See how the gallant ships dash together, and the monarchs of the forest bow their heads. And fire alone! Who shall stand against it when it devours its prey? But set wind and fire to work in hearty union! Remember the old city of London. When first the flames began it was utterly impossible to quench them because the wind fanned the flame, and the buildings gave way before the fire-torrent. Set the prairie on fire. If a rain-shower falls, and the air is still, the grass may perhaps cease to burn, but let the wind encourage the flame, and see how the devourer sweeps along while the tall grass is licked up by tongues of fire. We have lately read of forests on fire. What a sight! Hear how the mighty trees are crashing in the flame! What can stand against it! The fire setteth the mountains on a blaze. What a smoke blackens the skies; it grows dark at noon. As hill after hill offers up its sacrifice the timid imagine that the great day of the Lord has come. If we could see a spiritual conflagration of equal grandeur it were a consummation devoutly to be wished. O God, send us the Holy Ghost in this fashion: give us both the breath of spiritual life and the fire of unconquerable zeal, till nation after nation shall yield to the sway of Jesus. O thou who art our God, answer us by fire, we pray thee. Answer us both by wind and fire, and then shall we see thee to be God indeed. The kingdom comes not, and the work is flagging. O that thou wouldest send the wind and the fire! Thou wilt do this when we are all of one accord, all believing, all expecting, all prepared by prayer. Lord, bring us to this <u>waiting state</u>.

[Margin note: It's not about us]

II. Secondly, my brethren, follow me while I call your attention to THE IMMEDIATE EFFECTS of this descent of the Holy Spirit, for these symbols were not sent in vain. There were two immediate effects: the first was *filling*, and the second was *the gift of utterance*. I call special attention to the first, namely, filling: "It filled all the house where they were sitting": and it did not merely fill the house, but the men—"They were all filled with the Holy Ghost." When they stood up to speak even the ribald mockers in the crowd noticed this, for they said, "These men are full," and though they added "with new wine," yet they evidently detected a singular fulness about them. We are poor, empty things by nature, and useless while we remain so: we need to be filled with the Holy Ghost. Some people seem to believe in the Spirit of God giving utterance only, and they look upon instruction in divine things as of secondary importance. Dear, dear me, what trouble comes when we act upon that theory! How the empty vessels clatter, and rattle, and sound! Men in such case utter a wonderful amount of nothing, and even when that nothing is set on fire it does not come to much. I dread a revival of that sort, where the first thing and the last thing is everlasting talk. Those who set up for teachers ought to be themselves taught of the Lord; how can they communicate that which they have not received? Where the Spirit of God is truly at work he first fills and then gives utterance: that is his way. Oh that you and I were at this moment filled with the Holy Ghost. "Full!" Then they were not cold, and dead, and empty of life as we sometimes are. "Full." Then there was no room for anything else in any one of them! They were too completely occupied by the heavenly power to have room for the desires of the flesh. Fear was banished, every minor motive was expelled: the Spirit of God as it flooded their very being drove out of them everything that was extraneous. They had many faults and many infirmities before, but that day, when they were filled with the Spirit of God, faults and infirmities were no more perceptible. They became different men from what they had ever been before: men full of God are the reverse of men full of self. The difference between an empty man and a full man is something very wonderful. Let a thirsty person have an empty vessel handed to him. There may be much noise in the handing, but what a mockery it is as it touches his lips; but fill it with refreshing water, and perhaps there may be all the more silence in the passing it, for a full cup needs careful handling; but oh, what a blessing when it reaches the man's lips! Out of a full vessel he may drink his full. Out of a full church the world shall receive salvation, but never out of an empty one. The first thing we want as a church is to be filled with the Holy Ghost: the gift of utterance will then come as a matter of course. They ask me, "May the sisters speak anywhere? If not in the assembly, may they not speak in smaller meetings?" I answer, yes, if they are full of the Holy Ghost. Shall this brother or that be allowed to speak? Certainly, if he be filled, he may flow. May a layman preach? I know nothing about laymen except that I am no cleric myself; but let all speak who are full of the Holy Ghost. "Spring up, O well." If it be a fountain of living water who would restrain it, who could restrain it? Let him overflow who is full, <u>but mind he does not set up to pour out when there is nothing in him; for if he counts it his official duty to go pouring out, pouring out, pouring out, at unreasonable length, and yet nothing comes of it, I am sure he acts, not by the Holy Spirit, but according to his own vanity.</u>

The next Pentecostal symbol was *utterance*. As soon as the Spirit of God filled them they began to speak at once.

It seems to me that they began to speak before the people had come together. They could not help it; the inner forces demanded expression, and they must speak. So when the Spirit of God really comes upon a man, he does not wait till he has gathered an audience of the size which he desires, but he seizes the next opportunity. He speaks to one person, he speaks to two, he speaks to three, to anybody: he must speak, for he is full, and must have vent.

When the Spirit of God fills a man he speaks so as to be understood. The crowd spake different languages, and these Spirit-taught men spoke to them in the language of the country in which they were born. This is one of the signs of the Spirit's utterance. If my friend over yonder talks in a Latinized style to a company of costermongers, I will warrant you the Holy Ghost has nothing to do with him. If a learned brother fires over the heads of his congregation with a grand oration, he may trace his elocution, if he likes, to Cicero and Demosthenes, but do not let him ascribe it to the Holy Spirit, for that is not after his manner. The Spirit of God speaks so that his words may be understood, and if there be any obscurity it lies in the language used by the Lord himself.

The crowd not only understood, but they felt. There were lancets in this Pentecostal preaching, and the hearers "were pricked in the heart." The truth wounded men, and the slain of the Lord were many, for the wounds were in the most vital part. They could not make it out: they had heard speakers before, but this was quite a different thing. The men spake fire-flakes, and one hearer cried to his fellow, "What is this?" The preachers were speaking flame, and the fire dropped into the hearts of men till they were amazed and confounded.

Those are the two effects of the Holy Spirit,—a fulness of the Spirit in the ministry and the church, and next, a fire ministry, and a church on fire, speaking so as to be felt and understood by those around. Causes produce effects like themselves, and this wind and fire ministry soon did its work. We read that this "was noised abroad." Of course it was, because there had been a noise as of a rushing mighty wind. Next to that we read that all the people came together, and were confounded. There was naturally a stir, for a great wind from heaven was rushing. All were amazed and astonished, and while some enquired believingly, others began to mock. Of course they did: there was a fire burning, and fire is a dividing thing, and this fire began to separate between the precious and the vile, as it always will do when it comes into operation. We may expect at the beginning of a true revival to observe a movement among the people, a noise, and a stir. These things are not done in a corner. Cities will know of the presence of God, and crowds will be attracted by the event.

This was the immediate effect of the Pentecostal marvel, and I shall now ask you to follow me to my third point, which is this:—

III. The Holy Spirit being thus at work, what was THE MOST PROMINENT SUBJECT which these full men began to preach about with words of fire? Suppose that the Holy Spirit should work mightily in the church, what would our ministers preach about? We should have a revival, should we not, of the old discussions about predestination and free agency? I do not think so: these are happily ended, for they tended towards bitterness, and for the most part the disputants were not equal to their task. We should hear a great deal about the premillennial and the post-millennial advent, should we not? I do not think so. I never saw much of the Spirit of God in discussions or dreamings upon times and seasons which are not clearly revealed. Should we not hear learned essays upon advanced theology? No, sir; when the devil inspires the church we have modern theology; but when the Spirit of God is among us that rubbish is shot out with loathing. What did these men preach about? Their hearers said, "We do hear them speak in our own tongues the wonderful works of

God." Their subject was the wonderful works of God. Oh, that this might be to my dying day my sole and only topic,—"The wonderful works of God." For, first, they spoke of *redemption*, that wonderful work of God. Peter's sermon was a specimen of how they spoke of it. He told the people that Jesus was the Son of God, that they had crucified and slain him, but that he had come to redeem men, and that there was salvation through his precious blood. He preached redemption. Oh, how this land will echo again and again with "Redemption, redemption, redemption, redemption by the precious blood," when the Holy Ghost is with us. This is fit fuel for the tongue of flame: this is something worthy to be wafted by the divine wind. "God was in Christ, reconciling the world unto himself, not imputing their trespasses unto them." "The blood of Jesus Christ his Son cleanseth us from all sin." This is one of the wonderful works of God of which we can never make too frequent mention.

They certainly spoke of the next wonderful work of God, namely, *regeneration*. There was no concealing of the work of the Holy Spirit in that primitive ministry. It was brought to the front. Peter said, "Ye shall receive the Holy Ghost." The preachers of Pentecost told of the Spirit's work by the Spirit's power: conversion, repentance, renewal, faith, holiness, and such things were freely spoken of and ascribed to their real author, the divine Spirit. If the Spirit of God shall give us once again a full and fiery ministry we shall hear it clearly proclaimed, "Ye must be born again," and we shall see a people forthcoming which are born, not of blood, nor of the will of the flesh, but of the will of God, and by the energy which cometh from heaven. A Holy Ghost ministry cannot be silent about the Holy Ghost and his sacred operations upon the heart.

And very plainly they spoke on a third wonderful work of God, namely, *remission* of sin. This was the point that Peter pushed home to them, that on repentance they should receive remission of sins. What a blessed message is this;—Pardon for crimes of deepest dye, a pardon bought with Jesus' blood, free pardon, full pardon, irreversible pardon given to the vilest of the vile when they ground their weapons of rebellion, and bow at the feet that once were nailed to the tree. If we would prove ourselves to be under divine influence, we must keep to the divine message of fatherly forgiveness to returning prodigals. What happier word can we deliver?

These are the doctrines which the Holy Ghost will revive in the midst of the land when he worketh mightily—<u>redemption</u>, <u>regeneration</u>, <u>remission</u>. If you would have the Spirit of God resting on your labours, dear brothers and sisters, keep these three things ever to the front, and make all men hear in their own tongue the wonderful works of God.

IV. I shall close by noticing, in the fourth place, what were the GLORIOUS RESULTS of all this. Have patience with me, if you find the details somewhat long. The result of the Spirit coming as wind and fire, filling and giving utterance, was, first, in the hearers' *deep feeling*. There was never, perhaps, in the world such a feeling excited by the language of mortal man as that which was aroused in the crowds in Jerusalem on that day. You might have seen a group here, and a group there, all listening to the same story of the wondrous works of God, and all stirred and affected; for the heavenly wind and fire went with the preaching, and they could not help feeling its power. We are told that they were pricked in the heart. They had painful emotions, they felt wounds which killed their enmity. The word struck at the centre of their being: it pierced the vital point. Alas, people come into our places of worship nowadays to hear the preacher, and their friends ask them on their return, "How did you like him?" Was that your errand, to see how you liked him? What practical benefit is there in such a mode of using the servants of God? Are we sent among you to give opportunities for criticism? Yet the mass of men seem to think that we are nothing better than fiddlers or play-actors, who come upon the stage to help you while away an hour. O my hearers, if we are true to our God, and true to you, ours is a more solemn business than most men dream. The object of all true preaching is the heart: we aim at divorcing the heart from sin, and wedding it to Christ. Our ministry has failed, and has not the divine seal set upon it, unless it makes men tremble, makes them sad, and then anon brings them to Christ, and causes them to rejoice. Sermons are to be heard in thousands, and yet how little comes of them all, because the heart is not aimed at, or else the archers miss the mark. Alas, our hearers do not present their hearts as our target, but leave them at home, and bring us only their ears, or their heads. Here we need the divine aid. Pray mightily that the Spirit of God may rest upon all who speak in God's name, for then they will create deep feeling in their hearers!

Then followed an *earnest enquiry*. "They were pricked in their heart, and they said to Peter and the rest of the apostles, Men and brethren, <u>what shall we do</u>?" Emotion is of itself but a poor result unless it leads to practical action. To make men feel is well enough, but it must be a feeling which impels them to immediate movement, or at least to earnest enquiry as to what they shall do. O Spirit of God, if thou wilt rest on me, even me, men shall not hear and go their way and forget what they have heard! They will arise and seek the Father, and taste his love. If thou wouldst rest on all the brotherhood that publish thy word men would not merely weep while they hear, and be affected while the discourse lasts, but they would go their way to ask, "What must we do to be saved?" This is what we need. We do not require new preachers, but we need a new anointing of the Spirit. We do not require novel forms of service, but we want the fire Spirit, the wind Spirit to work by us till everywhere men cry, "What must we do to be saved?"

Then came *a grand reception of the word*. We are told that they gladly received the word, and they received it in two senses: first, Peter bade them repent, and so they did. They were pricked to the heart from compunction on account of what they had done to Jesus, and they sorrowed after a godly sort, and quitted their sins. They also believed in him whom they had slain, and accepted him as their Saviour there and then, without longer hesitancy. They trusted in him whom God had set forth to be a propitiation, and thus they fully received the word. Repentance and faith make up a complete reception of Christ, and they had both of these. Why should we not see this divine result to-day? We shall see it in proportion to our faith.

But what next? Why, they were *baptized* directly. Having repented and believed, the next step was to make confession of their faith; and they did not postpone that act for a single day; why should they? Willing hands were there, the whole company of the faithful were all glad to engage in the holy service, and that same day were they baptized into the name of the Father, and of the Son, and of the Holy Spirit. If the Holy Ghost were fully with us, we should never have to complain that many believers never confess their faith, for they would be eager to confess the Saviour's name in his own appointed way. Backwardness to be baptized comes too often of fear of persecution, indecision, love of ease, pride, or disobedience; but all these vanish when the heavenly wind and fire are doing their sacred work. Sinful diffidence soon disappears, sinful shame of Jesus is no more seen, and hesitancy and delay are banished for ever when the Holy Spirit works with power.

Furthermore, there was not merely this immediate confession, but as a result of the Spirit of God there was *great steadfastness.* "They continued steadfastly in the apostles' doctrine." We have had plenty of revivals of the human sort, and their results have been sadly disappointing. Under excitement nominal converts have been multiplied: but where are they after a little testing? I am sadly compelled to own that, so far as I can observe, there has been much sown, and very little reaped that was worth reaping, from much of that which has been called revival. Our hopes were flattering as a dream; but the apparent result has vanished like a vision of the night. But where the Spirit of God is really at work the converts stand: they are well rooted and grounded, and hence they are not carried about by every wind of doctrine, but they continue steadfast in the apostolic truth.

We see next that there was *abundant worship of God*, for they were steadfast not only in the doctrine, but in breaking of bread, and in prayer, and in fellowship. There was no difficulty in getting a prayer meeting then, no difficulty in maintaining daily communion then, no want of holy fellowship then; for the Spirit of God was among them, and the ordinances were precious in their eyes. "Oh," say some, "if we could get this minister or that evangelist we should do well." Brothers, if you had the Holy Spirit you would have everything else growing out of his presence, for all good things are summed up in him.

Next to this there came *striking generosity*. Funds were not hard to raise: liberality overflowed its banks, for believers poured all that they had into the common fund. Then was it indeed seen to be true that the silver and the gold are the Lord's. When the Spirit of God operates powerfully there is little need to issue telling appeals for widows and orphans, or to go down on your knees and plead for missionary fields which cannot be occupied for want of money. At this moment our village churches can scarcely support their pastors at a starvation rate; but I believe that if the Spirit of God will visit all the churches, means will be forthcoming to keep all going right vigorously. If this does not happen, I tremble for our Nonconformist churches, for the means of their existence will be absent; both as to spiritual and temporal supplies they will utterly fail. There will be no lack of money when there is no lack of grace. When the Spirit of God comes, those who have substance yield it to their Lord: those who have but little grow rich by giving of that little, and those who are already rich become happy by consecrating what they have. There is no need to rattle the box when the rushing mighty wind is heard, and the fire is dissolving all hearts in love.

Then came *continual gladness*. "They did eat their meat with gladness." They were not merely glad at prayer-meetings and sermons, but glad at breakfast and at supper. Whatever they had to eat they were for singing over it. Jerusalem was the happiest city that ever was when the Spirit of God was there. The disciples were singing from morning to night, and I have no doubt the outsiders asked, "What is it all about?" The temple was never so frequented as then; there was never such singing before; the very streets of Jerusalem, and the Hill of Zion, rang with the songs of the once despised Galileans.

They were full of gladness, and that gladness showed itself in *praising God*. I have no doubt they broke out now and then in the services with shouts of, "Glory! Hallelujah!" I should not wonder but what all propriety was scattered to the winds. They were so glad, so exhilarated that they were ready to leap for joy. Of course we never say "Amen," or "Glory!" now. We have grown to be so frozenly proper that we never interrupt a service in any way, because, to tell the truth, we are not so particularly glad, we are not so specially full of praise that we want to do anything of the sort. Alas, we have lost very much of the Spirit of God, and much of the joy and gladness which attend his presence, and so we have settled into a decorous apathy! We gather the pinks of propriety instead of the palm branches of praise. God send us a season of glorious disorder. Oh for a sweep of wind that will set the seas in motion, and make our ironclad brethren now lying so quietly at anchor to roll from stem to stern. As for us, who are as the little ships, we will fly before the gale if it will but speed us to our desired haven. Oh for fire to fall again,—fire which shall affect the most stolid! This is a sure remedy for indifference. When a flake of fire falls into a man's bosom he knows it, and when the word of God comes home to a man's soul he knows it too. Oh that such fire might first sit upon the disciples, and then fall on all around!

For, to close, there was then *a daily increase* of the church—"The Lord added to the church daily such as should be saved." Conversion was going on perpetually; additions to the church were not events which happened once a year, but they were everyday matters, "so mightily grew the word of God and prevailed." O Spirit of God, thou art ready to work with us to-day even as thou didst then! Stay not, we beseech thee, but work at once. Break down every barrier that hinders the incomings of thy might. Overturn, overturn, O sacred wind! Consume all obstacles, O heavenly fire, and give us now both hearts of flame and tongues of fire to preach thy reconciling word, for Jesus' sake. Amen.

2
THE SEALING OF THE SPIRIT

"In whom ye also trusted, after that ye heard the word of truth, the gospel of your salvation: in whom also after that ye believed, ye were sealed with that Holy Spirit of promise, which is the earnest of our inheritance until the redemption of the purchased possession, unto the praise of his glory."—Ephesians 1:13, 14.

~

I HAVE taken the whole passage for the sake of completing the sense, but I have no intention whatever of preaching upon all of it. Practically I only need for the topic of this morning the following words:—"In whom also after that ye believed, ye were sealed with that Holy Spirit of promise." The sealing of the Holy Spirit will be the subject of our meditation. There are many who have believed in the Lord Jesus Christ who are extremely anxious to obtain some token for good, some witness from God which shall render them quite sure that they are saved. They have not yet reached the full assurance of faith, and they feel uneasy till they attain it. They feel that these matters are too important to be left at all uncertain, and they, therefore, pine for some sure witness or seal. Men will not risk their estates, and no spiritually sensible man will endure to have his soul and its eternal affairs in jeopardy for an hour: hence this anxiety. It is true that by the way of faith only the fullest and best assurance may be reached, but many who do truly believe in the Lord Jesus Christ are not yet aware of this, and their trembling hearts crave for a testimonial from the infallible God to certify them that they are indeed saved. Yes, and I conceive that even more advanced saints, who know more fully where their standing is, and confess that they can only walk by faith, yet often sing with very great emphasis of desire—

> "Might I but hear thy heavenly tongue
>   But whisper *'Thou art mine,'*
> That cheerful word should raise my song
>   To notes almost divine."

Though we can and do believe, and can claim the privilege which belongs to those who have not seen and yet have believed, yet we would be glad to have a sight sometimes. We sometimes wish we could know by sure mark and evidence and token that our experience is after all a reality, and that we are indeed born of God.

> "O tell me that my worthless name
>   Is graven on thy hands!
> Show me some promise in thy book
>   Where my salvation stands!"

Now, in the best sense, this seal which we seek after is to be had; nay, it is manifestly seen by many of God's children. It does not supersede faith, but it rewards and strengthens it. There is a way by which God does speak to his own, and assure them that they are his; there is a pledge, and an earnest, and this is freely given to the people of God. May God's own Spirit enable me to speak aright upon this weighty subject.

The text says, "After that ye believed, ye were sealed with that Holy Spirit of promise;" and, therefore, first, I shall call your attention to *the position of this sealing*; secondly, to *the benefits which arise out of it*; and thirdly, to *the sealing itself*, which, indeed, I shall endeavour to explain all through.

I. First, let us speak of THE POSITION OF THIS SEALING. We are desirous to get some confirming seal from God set upon our souls, some sure token that we are indeed his own people. That sealing we can have, God does bestow it; but let us notice very carefully, lest we make a mistake, where that sealing comes in. *It does not come before believing.* According to the text it is "after that ye believed, ye were sealed." Now, there are hundreds of persons who are craving for something to see or to feel before they will believe in Jesus Christ; this is wickedness, and the result of an unbelief which is most offensive in the sight of God. If you demand a token before you believe, you practically say that you cannot take God's bare word for your comfort, that the sure word of testimony recorded in the Bible is not enough for you, that the solemn declaration of God may after all be false; at any rate, that you find it impossible to repose your confidence upon that alone, and must see something beside. If not a miracle, perhaps you demand a dream, or a strange feeling, or a mysterious operation; at any rate, if you do not see some sign and wonder, you declare that you will not believe. You do, in fact, say to God, "If thou wilt not go out of thy way to give me what I ask, and to do for me what I demand, then I will call thee a liar to thy face, by refusing to believe on thee." Ah, my hearer, this will not do; this is to provoke the Lord to jealousy, and he that doeth this shall receive no token whatsoever, except it be the sign of the unbelievers of Chorazin, for whom the day of judgment shall be more intolerable than for Sodom and Gomorrah.

Note also that this sealing *does not necessarily come at once with faith*. It grows out of faith, and comes "after that ye believed." We are not in every case sealed at the moment when we first trust in Jesus. I am persuaded that many who believe in Jesus enter into peace directly, and perceive at once the blessed assurance which is involved in their possessing the Holy Spirit; but with many others it is not so. I have frequently been asked this question, "What is a person to do who does believe in Jesus, but yet is not conscious of peace and joy, but is filled with such a conflict within that the utmost he can do is to cling to Jesus with trembling hope?" I have replied, "If you believe in Jesus Christ you are saved; the best evidence that you are saved lies in the assurance of the word of God that every believer has eternal life." Whether you *feel* that you are justified or not is not the point, you are to accept God's word, which assures you that every one that believeth is justified: you are bound to believe the testimony of God apart from the supporting evidence of inward experience, and if it were possible for you to be a believer by the year together, and yet to find no peace, still you would have no right to doubt what God says because you do not feel peace, but you are bound to hold on to God's promise whether you enjoy peace or not. My firm belief is that where there is a real faith in the promise of God, peace and the other fruits of the Spirit come as a necessary ultimate consequence, but even then they are not grounds of faith: the word of the Lord is the sole foundation upon which faith builds. Some people have a sort of confidence in God, but they are also looking out for confirming signs, and they spoil the simplicity of their faith by having one eye on Christ and another eye on their peace of mind. Now, my friend, this will never do. You are bound to believe in God as he is revealed in Christ Jesus unto salvation, altogether apart from peace, joy, or anything else. The witness of the Spirit within is not the ground nor the cause of our faith: faith cometh by hearing, and hearing by the word of God. I, being a sinner, believe that Jesus Christ came into the world to save sinners, and I rest my soul upon him, believing that he will save me; this is to be my standing, seal or no seal, token or no token. My dependence is not to be upon the seal of the Spirit, but upon the blood of the Son. The Spirit of God never takes the place of the Redeemer, he exercises his own peculiar office, which is to take of the things of Christ and show them unto us, and not to put his own things in the place of Jesus. <u>The foundation of our hope is laid in Christ from first to last, and if we rest there we are saved</u>. The seal does not always come with faith, but it follows after. I have said this because I am afraid lest in any way whatever you should leave the simple, plain, and solid ground of confidence in the finished work of Jesus Christ, and in that only. Recollect that a man who believes in Jesus Christ is as truly saved when he does not know it as he is when he does know it; <u>he is as truly the Lord's when he mourns in the valley of humiliation as when he sings on the mountain top of joy and fellowship</u>. Our ground of trust is not to be found in our experience, but in the person and work of our Lord Jesus.

> "I dare not trust the sweetest frame;
> But wholly lean on Jesus' name:
> On Christ the solid rock I stand,
> All other ground is sinking sand."

Note, also, as to the position of this sealing, that, while it is not the first, *it is not the last thing in the divine life*. It comes after believing, but when you obtain it there is something yet to follow. Perhaps you have had the notion that if you could once be told from the mouth of God himself that you were saved, you would then lie down and cease from life's struggle. It is clear, therefore, that such an assurance would be an evil thing for you, for a Christian is never more out of place than when he dreams that he has ceased from conflict. The natural, fit, and proper position for a soldier of Jesus Christ is to be at war with sin. We are wrestlers, and our normal condition is that of "striving according to his working who worketh in us mightily."

This side heaven, if there be a place for nest-building and ease-taking it is not the place for you: you are a pilgrim, and a pilgrim's business is to be on the road, pressing forward to the home beyond. Remember, if there be seats of ease, and no doubt there are, they are not for you, since you are a runner in a great race, with heaven and earth for witnesses. Cessation from watchfulness means ruin to your soul, the closing of conflict would show that you could never gain the victory, and perfect rest on earth would show that none remained for you in heaven. Even if the Spirit of God seal you, what will it amount to? To the inheritance itself, so that you can say, "I have attained perfection"? Certainly not. No, brethren, the Scripture says, "Which is *the earnest* of our inheritance till the redemption of the purchased possession." This side heaven all you cannot obtain is an earnest of the perfection of which heaven is made up.

"There rest shall follow toil,
And ease succeed to care:
The victors there divide the spoil;
They sing and triumph there."

Here we must labour, watch, run, fight, wrestle, agonise; all our forces, strengthened by the Eternal Spirit, must be expended in this high enterprise, striving to enter in at the strait gate: when we have obtained the sealing our warfare is not ended, we have only then received a foretaste of the victory, for which we must still fight on.

This is the true position of the sealing. It stands between the grace which enables us to believe, and the glory which is our promised inheritance.

II. We will notice, secondly, what are THE BENEFITS OF THIS SEALING, and while we are so doing, we shall be compelled to state what we think that sealing is, though that is to be the subject of the third head. The sealing spoken of in the text does not make the promises of God to be true. Please to notice that. This text has been preached upon as though it stated that the Spirit of God set his seal upon the gospel and the promises of God. Well, dear friends, it is true that the Spirit of God witnesses to the truth, and to the sureness of the promises, but that is evidently not intended here, for the text says, not that the promises were sealed, but that "ye were sealed." You are the writing which has the stamp put upon it; you yourselves are sealed. It is not even stated that the Spirit of God seals up covenant blessings as gold is sealed up in a bag, and reserves them for the chosen seed; the text tells us that believers themselves are thus reserved, and marked as the Lord's peculiar treasure, and it is upon believers themselves that this seal of the Holy Spirit is set. No, brethren, the Holy Spirit does not make the promises sure, they are sure of themselves; God that cannot lie has uttered them, and therefore they cannot fail. Nor, my brethren, does the Holy Spirit make sure our interest in those promises; that interest in the promises was sure in the divine decree, or ever the earth was, and is a matter of fact which cannot be changed. The promises are already sure to all the seed. *The Holy Spirit makes us sure that the word is true* and that we are concerned in it; but the promise was sure beforehand, and our interest in that promise was sure, too, from the moment in which it was bestowed upon us by the sovereign act of God.

To understand our text, you must notice that it is bounded by two words, "*In whom*," which two words are twice given in this verse. "In whom after that ye believed, ye were sealed." What is meant by "In whom"? The words signify "In Christ." It is *in Christ* that the people of God are sealed. We must therefore understand this sealing as it would relate to Christ, since so far, and so far only, can it relate to us. Was our Lord sealed? Turn to John 6:27, and there you have this exhortation: "Labour not for the meat which perisheth, but for that meat which endureth unto everlasting life, which the Son of Man shall give unto you: for *him hath God the Father sealed*." There is the clue to our text. "Him hath God the Father sealed:" for since our sealing is in him, it must be the same sealing.

Notice, then, first, that the ever-blessed Son was sealed on the Father's part *by God's giving a testimony* to him that he was indeed his own Son, and the sent one of the Lord. As when a king issues a proclamation, he sets his seal manual to it to say, "This is mine;" so when the Father sent his Son into the world, he gave him this testimony, "This is my beloved Son, in whom I am well pleased." He said this in words, but how did he give a perpetual testimony by a seal, which should be with him throughout life? It was by anointing him with the Holy Spirit. The seal that Jesus was the Messiah was that the Spirit of God rested upon him without measure. Hence we read expressions like these: "He was justified in the Spirit," "He was declared to be the Son of God with power, according to the Spirit of holiness by the resurrection from the dead." "It is the Spirit that beareth witness, because the Spirit is truth." Now, the Spirit of God, wherever it abides upon a man, is *the* mark that that man is accepted of God. We say not that where the Spirit merely strives at intervals there is any seal of divine favour, but where he abides it is assuredly so. The very fact that we possess the Spirit of God is God's testimony and seal in us that we are his, and that as he has sent his Son into the world, even so does he send us into the world.

Secondly, to our Lord Jesus Christ the Holy Spirit was a seal *for his own encouragement*. Our Lord condescended to restrain the power of his own Godhead, and as a servant he depended upon the Father for support. When he began his ministry he encouraged himself thus—"The Spirit of the Lord is upon me, because he hath sent me to bind up the broken-hearted." He found his stimulus of service, he found the authorisation of his service, he found his comfort and strength for service, in the fact that God had given him the Holy Spirit. This was his joy. Now, brothers and sisters, if we want to be encouraged for holy service by feeling quite sure that we are saved, where must we get that encouragement from? Read in the First Epistle of John, the third chapter and twenty-fourth verse, and there the seal of God is described—"Hereby we know that he abideth in us by the Spirit which he hath given us." Read also in the fourth chapter, verse 13, "Hereby know we that we dwell in him, because he hath given us of his Spirit." So that as the seal which comforted our Lord, and made him to know in times of depression that he was indeed beloved of the Father, was that he had the Spirit of God; so to you and to me, brethren, the possession of the Spirit of God is our continuous encouragement, for by this we may know beyond all question that we dwell in God and God dwelleth in us. The seal answers a two-fold purpose; it is on God's part a testimony, and to us an encouragement.

But the seal is meant to be *an evidence to others*. The Father set his seal upon his Son in order that others might discern that he was indeed sent of God. John says, "I knew him not: but he that sent me to baptize with water, the same said unto me, upon whom thou shalt see the Spirit descending, *and remaining* on him, the same is he which baptizeth with the Holy Ghost. And I saw, and bare record that this is the Son of God." The Spirit, then, was upon our Lord the seal for recognition; and, beloved, so must it be with us. We cannot be known by our fellow Christians except by the possession of the Spirit of God. Have you ever noticed how Peter claimed for the uncircumcised the rights of church membership in the fifteenth of Acts and the eighth and ninth verses? He says, "God, which knoweth the hearts, bare them witness, giving them the Holy Ghost, even as he did unto us; and put no difference between us and them, purifying their hearts by faith": so that to Peter the possession of the Holy Spirit was the broad seal of heaven which the Lord never sets upon a heart wherein there is no faith. The same argument had been felt in all its power by him when he said, "Can any man forbid water, that these should not be baptized which have received the Holy Ghost as well as we?" Paul used this as his test concerning the sons of men; for in Romans 8:9, he says, "Ye are not in the flesh, but in the Spirit, if so be that the Spirit of God dwell in you. Now, if any man have not the Spirit of Christ he is none of his;" plainly indicating that the absence of the Spirit is fatal, for the divine signature is not at the bottom of the document; but if the Spirit of God be there, then all is right, for the Lord never puts his seal to anything which is not sound and true. Rest quite sure that where the Spirit of God abides there the gospel of Jesus Christ has been written on the heart, and the man is saved.

Further, the fourth effect of the seal upon Christ was that *it was to the world a witness.* The Spirit of God upon Jesus Christ was not recognised by the ungodly world to be indeed divine, but they perceived and were astonished at a something about him which they did not understand. He spake with authority and not as the scribes, and they confessed "Never man spake like this man." They did not know what spirit he was of, but they knew they hated it, and straightway they began to oppose him. Now, brothers and sisters, if you have the same seal as your Lord, which is described in the text as "the Spirit of promise," the same result will follow: men will wonder at you, misunderstand you, and oppose you. And what is the reason? Never in this world did the Spirit of promise appear without opposition from the spirit of bondage. Isaac was the child of promise, and did not Ishmael, who was born after the flesh, persecute him? The two seeds, of the flesh and of the promise, are at daggers drawing with each other. When the Lord sets his seal upon you by giving you the Spirit of promise, so that you are not under the law but under Christ, the world will know it; they will not admire you, but they will strive against you to destroy you.

Once more, the seal upon our Lord Jesus Christ was intended for a fifth reason, namely—*for his perseverance even to the end.* A seal is set upon a treasure which we mean to preserve; and so was the precious Redeemer sealed. Now, you will say to me, "But dare we speak of Jesus Christ as being preserved by the Spirit of God?" My dear brethren, we must never forget the wonderful self-denial of Christ in that he laid aside his own divine power, and while he was in this world he said the Father was greater than he, and he became a man so as to pray, and to believe, and to depend upon the Father. Jesus Christ put himself into such a condition while he was here that he relied upon the Spirit of God to uphold him. Do you doubt it? Turn to the forty-second of Isaiah, and you there get it in express words: "Behold my servant whom I uphold!" See how he puts himself, as a servant, to be upheld by the Lord. "Mine elect, in whom my soul delighteth. I have put my Spirit upon him: he shall bring forth judgment to the Gentiles: he shall not cry nor lift up, nor cause his voice to be heard in the street: a bruised reed shall he not break, and the smoking flax shall he not quench: he shall bring forth judgment unto truth." There can be no doubt that this is Christ; for these very words are quoted concerning himself. Now, what comes of the upholding of the blessed Spirit? "He shall not fail nor be discouraged until he hath set judgment in the earth, and the isles shall wait for his law." So that the Spirit of God upheld Christ, and sustained him, and kept him, till his life's work was finished, without his failing or being discouraged. My brethren, this is how you and I must be kept; this is the seal which we need, which shall preserve us as the consecrated ones of God, so that when he cometh, he shall find us under seal and safe.

Let me now recapitulate. Upon our Lord Jesus the Spirit of God acted as a seal, namely, as God's testimony that he was his Son, as an encouragement to his own heart, as an evidence to others, as a witness to the world, and as a help to perseverance, even to the end. The like benefits will the sealing of the Spirit confer upon us: "in Christ Jesus after that ye believed, ye were sealed with that holy

Spirit of promise."

III. Thirdly, let us consider THE SEALING ITSELF. A great deal has been said on this point which has tended to foster superstition. Some have supposed that there is a separate act of the Spirit of God in which he seals believers. It may be so, I will not raise the question; but I should be very sorry if any man here, living in sin, should nevertheless look back upon some time of religious excitement or enjoyment and say, "I am safe, for on that occasion I was sealed;" and I should be very sorry to have any brother take as the sure reason why he is saved some remarkable experience which he underwent on a certain day long past. A seal is for the present, and is not a mere memory, but an object palpable *now*, and before the eyes. I am afraid many have been deceived into carelessness by the notion of a sealing received long ago. Let us seek out the truth. According to the text, as far as I can read it, here is a man who has believed in Jesus, and he desires a seal that God loves him: God gives him the Spirit, and that is all the seal he can wish for or expect. Nothing more is wanted, nothing else would be so good. The very fact that the Spirit of God works in you to will and to do according to God's good pleasure, is your seal; you do not require anything beyond. I do not say that any one operation of the Holy Spirit is to be regarded as the seal, but the whole of them together, as they prove his being within us, make up that seal. It is better, however, to keep to the doctrine that the Spirit of God in the believer is himself the seal.

> "Thou art the earnest of his love,
>   The pledge of joys to come,
> And thy soft wings, celestial dove,
>   Will safe convey me home."

Now, let us look at what the context tells us about this. If you read on, the apostle tells us that *wisdom and revelation* in the knowledge of God are part of the seal. Kindly turn to the chapter and follow out the apostle's line of argument. He says, (verse 15), "Wherefore I also, after I heard of your faith, etc., cease not to give thanks for you, making mention of you in my prayers; that the God of our Lord Jesus Christ, the Father of glory, may give unto you the spirit of wisdom and revelation in the knowledge of him." See, then, if ye have believed in Jesus Christ the Spirit of God comes upon you, and he gives you wisdom and revelation. Doctrines in the Word which you never understood before become clear to you—"the eyes of your understanding being enlightened;" the blessings promised are more distinctly discerned, and you see "the hope of your calling, and the riches of the glory of the Lord's inheritance in the saints." The deeper truths, which at first quite staggered and puzzled you, gradually open up to you, and you see and appreciate them. More especially you discover the glory of Christ and see the exceeding greatness of the power with which the Lord works in the saints "according to the working of his mighty power, which he wrought in Christ, when he raised him from the dead, and set him at his own right hand in the heavenly places, far above all principality, and power, and might, and dominion, and every name that is named, not only in this world, but in that which is to come." You drink deep into the blessed thought that Jesus is the head over all things to his church, and you obtain some glimpses into the mysterious doctrine that the church "is his fulness, the fulness of him that filleth all in all." Now, brethren, if we know these things aright the Spirit has taught us, and the consequence of it is that we say to ourselves, "Certainly I must be a child of God, for I never understood the things of God before." How could I have learned them if I had not been taught of God. The Master seems to stand by our side and say, "Blessed art thou, Simon Bar-Jona: for flesh and blood hath not revealed it unto thee, but my Father which is in heaven." If you have been made to see the abounding grace of God, the grandeur of the plan of salvation, and the choice beauties of the blessed person of

Jesus Christ, you have a sure seal upon your soul, for like the blind man in the gospels you can say, "One thing I know, whereas I was blind now I see."

Following on to the next chapter you will see that the Spirit of God works in every man who possesses him *life*, and that life becomes another form of the seal. "You hath he quickened who were dead in trespasses and sin." That life is of a new kind, and has a renewing power, so that men forsake the course of this world, and no longer fulfil the desires of the flesh and of the mind. This new life they trace to God, who is rich in mercy, who in his great love wherewith he loved them, even when they were dead in sins, hath quickened them together with Christ. They trace this life entirely to the grace of God,—"by grace are ye saved"; and they see that this life produces in them good works, "for we are his workmanship, created in Christ Jesus unto good works." I need not explain how this life uplifts us to sit in the heavenlies with Christ, for most of you know all about it; you have received a life from above, a living and incorruptible seed is in you, you have passed into a new world, you have feelings, desires, fears, hopes, such as you never knew before, and thus your outward life is also changed, so that you follow after that which is according to the will of God. Now, brethren, what can be a better seal to you that you are indeed saved than this life which you feel within. <u>This is the way in which the Spirit of God seals you, by making you partakers of the divine life, which never did reside in the unbeliever yet, and never can dwell apart from faith.</u> To "as many as received him, to them gave he power to become the sons of God, even to as many as believed on his name." "He that believeth on the Son hath everlasting life: and he that believeth not the Son shall not see life; but the wrath of God abideth on him." So that wisdom and life, which are both sure results of the indwelling of the Spirit of God, are a seal to us that we are really saved.

Go on a little further and you will notice upon the one

seal a further mark, namely—*fellowship*. "Ye were without Christ, being aliens from the commonwealth of Israel, and strangers from the covenants of promise, having no hope, and without God in the world: but now in Christ Jesus ye who sometimes were far off are made nigh by the blood of Christ. For he is our peace, who hath made both one, and hath broken down the middle wall of partition between us." Those who have believed in Jesus Christ are led by the Spirit of God to love their fellow Christians, and thus "we know that we have passed from death unto life, because we love the brethren." Once we thought the godly a dull and melancholy set, at any rate we let them go their own way, and we were glad to keep aloof from them; but now we delight in their society, sympathize with their pursuits, and are willing to share their persecutions. We count the saints of God the best company in the world; we would sooner sit down and talk half an hour with a poor, bed-ridden Christian woman, than be found in the courts of princes. This brotherly love becomes a seal of grace within our hearts, for John tells us in his first epistle, "every one that loveth is born of God, and knoweth God." "If we love one another, God dwelleth in us, and his love is perfected in us." 1 John 4:7, 12.

Even more striking is that which follows, namely, that we have *fellowship with God*. The apostle speaks of us as reconciled unto God by the cross, by which the enmity is slain, and he says of our Lord, "Through him we both have access by one Spirit unto the Father." I am following the course of the chapter. When you and I feel that we commune with God, that there is no quarrel between him and us, that he is loved of us as we are loved of him, that we can draw near to him in prayer and speak to him, that he hears us and deigns to grant us gracious answers of peace, these are blessed seals of salvation. Some of us can look back on times of fellowship with God, on seasons of prevailing prayer with him, and upon countless answers to our petitions: all these become to us infallible tokens of divine love.

I shall not tire you if I bid you notice for one moment that the apostle puts in next *upbuilding*,—"And are built upon the foundation of the apostles and prophets, Jesus Christ himself being the chief corner stone; in whom all the building fitly framed together groweth unto an holy temple in the Lord." Are you not conscious, believers, that you are being built up unto a divinely glorious form, after a high and noble model? It doth not yet appear what we shall be, but you must be conscious that course upon course of precious stones have been builded upon the foundation of your faith in Christ. Since you have known the Lord you have made a distinct advance. At times you are afraid you have only grown downwards, but you have grown; there is a something about you now which was not there ten years ago. I am distinctly conscious, somehow, that twenty years ago I was not what I now am. I sometimes feel like a bird in the eggshell! I am chipping it away bit by bit, I believe it will break one of these days, and the bird will come out; but I often feel my wings fretted and cramped by the shell; I want the life in me to be developed and set free. Do you never feel the same? Have you not felt as if you yourself were big with a far more glorious nature, and longed for deliverance from flesh and frailty. These groanings, aspirations, hopes, and desires are all seals of salvation; you will never find the ungodly thus moved. These pangs are peculiar to life. You are not a finished structure, but a house in process of erection, and you may be sure that one of these days the topstone shall be brought forth with shoutings of "Grace, grace unto it." But this upbuilding through the Spirit of God is the seal of the Spirit; it is to you the evidence that God has begun a good work in you, and is carrying it on.

Last of all, the second chapter finishes up by saying, "In whom ye also are builded together for an habitation of God through the Spirit;" and this seems to me to gather up all that I have said before. The *indwelling* of the Spirit in the saints, in the whole of them united, and in each one in particular, is a choice seal.

> "Dost thou not dwell in all the saints,
> And seal them heirs of heaven?"

Yes, that is the manner of the sealing, according to the prayer of our hymn—

> "Jesus, my Lord, reveal
> In charms of grace divine,
> And be thyself the sacred seal,
> That pearl of price is mine."

If you have the Spirit of God dwelling in you, you must be the Lord's. Will the Spirit of God dwell in any temple but that which God has consecrated? He may come upon men to strive with them for awhile, but he will never *dwell* in any heart that has not been cleansed with the blood of Jesus, nor can he possibly reside permanently in any soul which is defiled with self-righteousness and love of sin. No, beloved, if the Spirit of God dwell in you, you want no dreams, nor angels' whispers, nor noises in the air. The indwelling Spirit is the only seal you need. I put it to you, brothers and sisters, what more do you want? What more could God give you? Suppose you were to meet on the road home, standing on the snow, an angel, clothed in glittering white, and that he should say to you, "I have a message from God to you"—should then mention your name and add, "You are one of God's chosen." That vision would comfort you for half-an-hour, I have no doubt, but many desponding spirits would not be comforted much longer, for the devil would say, "It was snowing? No doubt the flakes blew into your eyes; or else you have a fine imagination." "Oh, but," you would say, "I heard him speak." "Ah, you had noises in your head; you are becoming a fair subject for Bedlam." I confess if you were to tell me the story, I should not make any bones about it, but should say, "You are not such a fool as to believe that, are you?" and you would find many other people of the same mind. Now there can be no doubt about the seal of the text. You have been taught of God what no one but the Spirit of God could have taught you; you have a life in you which no one but the Spirit could have given you: of that knowledge and that life you are perfectly conscious; you do not want to ask anybody else about them. A man may ask me whether I know so and so; but I am the best witness whether I do or not. If I am asked, "How do you know you are alive?" Well, I walk about, that is all; but I am quite sure about it, and I do not want any further evidence.

The best seal to a man's heart must be that of which he is conscious, and about which he needs not appeal to others. Give me a seal that is as sure as my own existence: I fail to see how God himself can give me anything more sure than the the gift of his Spirit working knowledge and life in me. "Oh," says one, "but if I could hear a voice." Suppose you did. Then the argument of fear would be that there are countless voices, and one may be mistaken for another. You were in the street when you heard it; perhaps it was a parrot or a starling in the upper window. Who knows? It is so easy for the ear to be deceived. Many a time you have said, "I know I heard so and so," when you did not hear it, but something very like it. I would not believe my own ears, if their evidence had to do with my soul, one half so readily as I would believe my own consciousness. Since knowledge and life and other things I have mentioned just now, are all matters of consciousness, they are much better seals than anything could be which appealed like an angelic vision to the eye, or like a mysterious voice to the ear. Here you have something sure and steadfast. If the Spirit of God dwell in you you are his, and if he dwell not in you you are none of his.

Take this for the closing word, "Grieve not the Spirit of God, whereby ye are sealed unto the day of redemption," but love him, honour him, and obey him; so will the seal always be bright before your eyes.

As to you who have not believed, I conclude with this sentence.—Do not ask for seals; you have nothing to do with seals, but with Jesus. "An evil and adulterous generation seeketh after a sign." Believe in Christ Jesus, and when you have trusted him, then shall there come signs, seals, marks. God bless you, for Christ's sake. Amen.

3
THE SPIRIT OF BONDAGE AND ADOPTION

"For ye have not received the spirit of bondage again to fear; but ye have received the Spirit of adoption, whereby we cry, Abba, Father. The Spirit itself beareth witness with our spirit, that we are the children of God."—Romans 8:15, 16.

~

THESE two verses are full of the word "spirit," and they are also full of spiritual truth. We have read in previous verses about the flesh and of the result that comes of minding it, namely, death. But now, in this verse, we get away from the flesh, and think only of the work of the Holy Spirit upon our spirits, and of the blessed privilege which comes of it—"that we should be called the sons of God." We cannot enter into this except by the power of the Holy Spirit, for spiritual truth must be spiritually discerned: our eyes need God's light, and our spirits need the Holy Spirit's quickening. We breathe our prayer to the Great Spirit that he would make us feel the full meaning of his word.

I think that I see in the text the fourfold work of the Spirit: first, *the spirit of bondage*; secondly, *the spirit of adoption*;

thirdly, *the spirit of prayer*,—here it is, "Whereby we cry." And fourthly, *the spirit of witness*. "The Spirit itself beareth witness with our spirit, that we are the children of God."

I. Consider, first of all, THE SPIRIT OF BONDAGE. *Much of the bondage in which we are plunged by our fallen nature is not the work of the Spirit of God at all.* Bondage under sin, bondage under the flesh, bondage to the fashions and customs of the world, bondage under the fear of man,—this is carnal bondage, the work of the flesh, and of sin, and of the devil. But there is a sense of bondage, to which, I think, the apostle here mainly alludes, which is of the Spirit of God. Before the Spirit of God within us becomes the Spirit of liberty, he is, first of all, the Spirit of bondage. The Spirit is not first a quickening Spirit to us, but a withering Spirit:—"The grass withereth, the flower fadeth: because the Spirit of the Lord bloweth upon it: surely the people is grass." The divine Spirit wounds before he heals, he kills before he makes alive. We usually draw a distinction between law-work and gospel-work; but law-work is the work of the Spirit of God, and is so far a true gospel-work that it is a frequent preliminary to the joy and peace of the gospel. The law is the needle, which draws after it the silken thread of blessing, and you cannot get the thread into the stuff without the needle: men do not receive the liberty wherewith Christ makes them free till, first of all, they have felt bondage within their own spirit driving them to cry for liberty to the great Emancipator, the Lord Jesus Christ. This sense or spirit of bondage works for our salvation by leading us to cry for mercy.

Let us notice that *there is a kind of bondage which is, in part at least, the work of the Spirit of God*, although it is often darkened, blackened, and made legal in a great measure by other agencies which do not aim at our benefit. That part of the bondage which I shall now describe is altogether the work of the Spirit of God. That is, first, *when men are brought into bondage through being convinced of sin*. This bondage is not the work of nature; certainly, never the work of the devil.

It is not the work of human oratory, nor of human reason; it is the work of the Spirit of God; as it is written, "When the Spirit of truth is come, he shall convince the world of sin." It needs a miracle to make a man know that he is in very deed a sinner. He will not own it. He kicks against it. Even when he confesses the outward transgression, he does not know or feel the inward heinousness of his guilt, so as in his soul to be stunned, and confounded, and humbled, by the fact that he is a rebel against his God. Now, no man can ever know a Saviour without knowing himself a sinner: even as no man can value a physician while he is ignorant of the existence and evil of disease. By the killing sentence of the law we are bruised, and broken, and crushed to atoms, as to all comeliness and self-righteousness. This, I say, is the work of the Spirit of God; he worketh a necessary spirit of bondage within us by putting us under a sense of sin.

The Spirit of God is always the Spirit of truth, and therefore he only convinces men of that which is true: he puts them into no false, or fanciful, or needless bondage. "When the Spirit of truth is come, he shall convince the world of sin,"—because it is sinful. When the Spirit puts men into bondage because they are sinners, he only puts them into their right place. When he came to some of us by the law he made us feel what we were by nature; and what we felt and saw was the truth. He made us see things as they really were. Until he came, we put bitter for sweet and sweet for bitter, darkness for light and light for darkness; but when the Spirit of truth was come, then sin appeared sin. Then we were in bondage, and it was no fancied slavery, but the very truth.

The Spirit of God also brought us farther into bondage when he *made us feel the assurance that punishment must follow upon sin*, when he made us know that God can by no means clear the guilty, and that he was not playing with us when he said, "The soul that sinneth, it shall die." We were made to feel the sentence of death in ourselves, that we might not trust in ourselves. At that time we trembled on the brink of fate. We wondered that we were not already in hell. We were so convinced of sin that it was a matter of astonishment to us that the sentence did not immediately take place upon us. We were speechless before God, as to excuse or justification. We could not offer anything by which we could turn away the edge of justice, though we saw it like a glittering sword stripped of the scabbard of almighty patience. Do you know what this means? I can hardly hope that you will prize the atonement, or feel the sweetness of the expiation by blood, unless, first of all, you have felt that your soul's life was due to God on account of your transgressions. We must know a shutting-up under the sentence of the law, or we shall never rejoice in the liberty which comes to us by grace through the blood of the Lamb of God. Blessed be the Spirit of God for working in us this double sense of bondage, first making us know that we are guilty, and, secondly, making us feel that the justice of God must punish us for sin.

And then, further, the Spirit of God operates as a spirit of bondage upon the hearts of those whom God will save, by bringing them to *feel the utter impossibility of their hoping to clear themselves by the works of the law.* We heard this sentence thundered in our soul—"By the deeds of the law there shall no flesh be justified in his sight: for by the law is the knowledge of sin." We could not meet our God under the law: we looked up to Sinai's fiery summit, whereon the Lord revealed himself, and we felt that its crags were too steep for our tottering feet to climb. Even if the way were smooth, how could we dare to pass through the thick darkness, and hold communion with Jehovah, who is a consuming fire? The Spirit of God once for all weaned us from all thought of a righteousness of our own. We were clean divorced from the legal spirit, and compelled to abhor the very notion of justifying ourselves in the sight of a pure and holy God by our works, or feelings, or prayers. This was the work of the Spirit of God.

This result is always produced in every child of God, but not always by the same degree of bondage. Fetters of different weights are used in this prison-house, as wisdom and prudence appoint. The spirit of bondage comes not to all alike; for some find peace and life in a moment, and come to Calvary as soon as Sinai begins to thunder.

I have known this spirit of bondage come with great force to men who have been open transgressors. Others who have been kept by the preventing grace of God from the extremes of open sin have not felt so much of it; but men that have blasphemed God, broken the Sabbath, and violated every holy thing,—when they are brought before God under a sense of sin, have frequently had a hard time of it. See how Saul was three days blinded, and did neither eat nor drink. Read John Bunyan's "Grace Abounding," and notice the five years of his subjection to this spirit of bondage. It must in his case be noted that his bondage was far from being altogether the work of the Spirit, for much of it arose from his own unbelief. But still there was in the core and heart of it a work of the Spirit of God most wonderfully convincing him of sin. I should not wonder if some of my hearers, who may have gone far into outward transgression, are made to feel, when brought to spiritual life, great grief and humiliation under a sense of their sin.

Such bondage often happens to those who, as the old authors used to say, were "close sinners"—men who did not even know that they were sinners at all, but, in consequence of their morality and the strictness of their lives, had a high conceit of their own excellence in the sight of God. Certain of these people experience most fearful convictions of sin: as if God would say to each one, "I must rid thee of thy self-righteousness. I must cure thee of trusting in thy moral life; and therefore I will let thee see into the depths of thy depravity. I will discover to thee thy sins against light and knowledge, thy sins against conscience, thy sins against the love of God. Thou shalt be brought into sore bondage; but that bondage shall heal thee of thy pride."

I have noticed one thing more, and that is, that those who are in after life to be greatly useful are often thus digged, and tilled, and dunged, in order that much fruit may be brought forth by them in after years. I have had to deal with as many troubled souls as any living man, and God has greatly used me for their deliverance; but this never could have happened, so far as I can judge, unless I had myself been the subject of a terrible law-work, convincing me not only of my actual sin, but of the source of that sin, namely, a deep and bottomless fountain of depravity in my own nature. When I have met with persons driven to despair, and almost ready to destroy themselves, I have said, "Yes, I understand all that: I have been in those sepulchral chambers, and can sympathize with those who are chilled by their damps. I know the heart of a stranger, for I also was a captive in Egypt, and worked at the brick-kilns." In such a case this bondage of spirit becomes a profitable preparation for after work. The sword that has to cut through coats of mail must be annealed in many fires; it must endure processes which a common blade escapes. Do not, therefore, all of you expect that the spirit of bondage will be seen in you to the same degree; for, after all, it is not the spirit of bondage which is to be desired for its own sake, but that which comes after it—the Spirit of liberty in Christ Jesus.

Our text reminds us that *the result of this spirit of bondage in the soul is fear*:—"The spirit of bondage to fear." There are five sorts of fears, and it is well always to distinguish between them.

There is the natural fear which the creature has of its Creator, because of its own insignificance and its Maker's greatness. From that we shall never be altogether delivered; for with holy awe we shall bow before the divine majesty, even when we come to be perfect in glory.

Secondly, there is a carnal fear: that is, the fear of man. May God deliver us from it! May we never cease from duty because we dread the eye of man! Who art thou that thou shouldst be afraid of a man, that shall die? From this cowardice God's Spirit delivers believers.

The next fear is a servile fear—the fear of a slave towards his master, lest he should be beaten when he has offended. That is a fear which should rightly dwell in every unregenerate heart. Until the slave is turned into a child he ought to feel that fear which is suitable to his position. By means of this fear the awakened soul is driven and drawn to Christ, and learns the perfect love which casts it out.

If servile fear be not cast out it leads to a fourth fear, namely, a diabolical fear; for we read of devils, that they "believe and tremble." This is the fear of a malefactor towards the executioner, such a fear as possesses souls that are shut out for ever from the light of God's countenance.

But, fifthly, there is a filial fear which is never cast out of the mind. This is to be cultivated. This is "the fear of the Lord" which is "the beginning of wisdom." This is a precious gift of grace: "Blessed is the man that feareth the Lord." This makes the saints fearful of offending, lest they should grieve infinite love; it causes them to walk before the Lord with the fear of a loving child who would not in anything displease his parent.

When the spirit of bondage is at work upon the heart, there is much of the fourth form of fear, namely, servile fear; and I tell you that it is the Spirit of truth which brings this to us, because we are in a condition which demands it: we are slaves until Christ sets us free, and, being still under the law, servile fear is our most natural and proper feeling. Would you have the bondsman rejoice in a liberty which he does not possess? Is he not the more likely to be free if he loathes his slavery? I wish that every man here, who is not a child of God, would become possessed with servile fear, and tremble before the Most High.

Now, mark that *while this fear lasts it is intended to work us toward God*. I have already touched upon that. This bondage, which causes fear, breaks us off from self-righteousness; it makes us value the righteousness of Christ, and it also puts an end to certain sins. Many a man, because he is afraid of the consequences, leaves off this and that which would have ruined him; and, so far, the fear is useful to him; and, in after life, the sense of the terror which fear wrought in his soul, will keep him nearer to his Lord. How can he return to that evil thing which aforetime filled his soul with bitterness and grief?

But now I want to notice that *in due time we outgrow this bondage, and never receive it again*, for "We have not received the spirit of bondage again to fear." There comes a time when the Spirit of truth no longer causes bondage. Why not? Because we are not slaves any longer, and therefore there is no bondage for us. Because we are no longer guilty, having been cleared in the court of God, and therefore no sin should press upon our spirit. Because we are made to be the children of God; and God forbid that God's children should tremble like slaves. No, we have not received the spirit of bondage again, for the Spirit of God has not brought it to us again; and though the devil tries to bring it we do not "receive" his goods; and though sometimes the world thinks that we ought to feel it, we are not of the world, and we will not "receive" the world's spirit. We are new creatures in Christ Jesus; we are not under the law, but under grace; and therefore we are free from our former bondage. "We have not received the spirit of bondage again to fear." I know some Christians, or persons who call themselves so, who often come under this spirit of bondage. They erroneously say, "If I have sinned I have ceased to be a child of God." That is the spirit of bondage with a vengeance. If a servant disobeys he will be sent adrift; but you cannot discharge your child. My son is my son for ever; who denies that? Sonship is a settled fact, and never can be altered under any possible circumstances. If I am a child of God, who shall separate me from the love of God which is in Christ Jesus, my Lord? Some perform all religious actions from a principle of fear; and they abstain from this and that iniquity because of fear. A child of God does not desire to be thus driven or held back. He works not for reward; he toils not in order to gain salvation. He is saved; and because God has "worked in him to will and to do of his own good pleasure," therefore he works out the salvation which God has already worked in. Blessed is the man who knows that he is no longer a servant, but has become an heir of God, a joint-heir with Jesus Christ.

II. This brings us to our second head, which is, THE SPIRIT OF ADOPTION. I should require a week to preach properly upon that blessed theme. Instead of preaching upon it, I will give you hints.

Will you kindly notice that the apostle said, "Ye have not received the spirit of bondage"? If he had kept strictly to language he would have added, "But ye have received the Spirit of"—what? Why of "*liberty*." That is the opposite of bondage. Ay, but our apostle is not to be hampered by the rigid rules of composition. He has inserted a far greater word:—"Ye have received the Spirit of *adoption*." This leads me to observe that, from this mode of putting it, it is clear that the Spirit of adoption is in the highest sense the spirit of liberty. If the Son make you free, ye shall be free indeed. If ye yourselves become sons through that blessed Son, oh, the freeness of your spirits! Your soul has nothing now to fear; you need not dread the wrath of God, for he has sworn, "I would not be wroth with thee, nor rebuke thee." The believer feels the love of God shed abroad within him, and therefore he exercises a liberty to draw nigh to God, such as he never had before. He has access with boldness: he learns to speak with God as a child speaks to a father. See what a blessed thing is this Spirit of liberty, this Spirit of *adoption*.

Now, the apostle said, "Ye have not received the spirit of bondage again to fear." What is the opposite of that?

He should have added—should he not?—"but ye have received the Spirit of liberty by which ye have *confidence.*" He has not in so many words expressed himself thus, but he has said all that and a great deal more by saying, "Whereby we cry, Abba, Father." This is the highest form of confidence that can be thought of,—that a child of God should be able, even when he is forced to cry, to cry nothing less than, "Abba, Father." At his lowest, when he is full of sorrow and grief, even in his cryings and lamentings, he sticks to "Abba, Father." This is a joyous confidence indeed! Oh, that God may give it to you, dearly beloved, to the very full!

Thus it is clear that the Spirit of adoption is a spirit of liberty, and a spirit of confidence. As a child is sure that its father will love him, feed him, clothe him, teach him, and do all that is good for him, so are we sure that "No good thing will he withhold from them that walk uprightly;" but he will make all things to "work together for good to them that love God."

The spirit of bondage made us fear, but the Spirit of adoption gives us *full assurance*. That fear which distrusts God—that fear which doubts whether he will remain a loving and merciful God—that fear which makes us think that all his love will come to an end—that is gone, for we cry, "Abba, Father," and that cry is the death of doubting and fearing. We sing to brave music, "I know whom I have believed, and am persuaded that he is able to keep that which I have committed unto him."

The Spirit of adoption, moreover, is a spirit of *gratitude*. Oh, that ever the Lord should put *me* among the children! Why should he do this? He did not want for children that he should adopt *me*. The First-born alone was enough to fill the Father's heart throughout eternity. And yet the Lord puts *us* among the children. Blessed be his name for ever and ever! "Behold, what manner of love the Father hath bestowed upon us, that we should be called the sons of God!"

The Spirit of adoption is a spirit of *child-likeness*. It is pretty, though sometimes sad, to see how children imitate their parents. How much the little man is like his father! Have you not noticed it? Do you not like to see it, too? You know you do. Ay, and when God gives the Spirit of adoption, there begins in us, poor fallen creatures as we are, some little likeness to himself; and that will grow to his perfect image. We cannot become God; but we have the privilege and the power to become the sons of God. "Even to as many as believe on his name" does Jesus give this privilege; and therefore we grow up into him in all things, who is our Head, and at the same time the pattern and mirror of what all the children of God are to be.

Thus, dear friends, let us see with great joy that we have not received again the spirit of bondage. We shall not receive it any more. The Spirit of God will never come to us in that form again, for now we have been washed in the blood, we have been taken away from being heirs of wrath even as others, we have been placed in the family of the Most High, and we feel the Spirit of adoption within us, whereby we cry, "Abba, Father."

III. Just two or three words only upon the next spirit, which is, THE SPIRIT OF PRAYER. Whenever the Spirit of adoption enters into a man it sets him praying. He cannot help it. He does not wish to help it.

> "Prayer is the Christian's vital breath,
>   The Christian's native air;
> His watchword at the gates of death:
>   He enters heaven with prayer."

And this praying of the true believer who has the Spirit of adoption is very *earnest* praying, for it takes the form of crying. He does not *say*, "Abba, Father." Anybody can say those words. But he *cries*, "Abba, Father." Nobody can *cry*, "Abba, Father," but by the Holy Ghost. When those two words, "Abba, Father," are set to the music of a child's cry, there is more power in them than in all the orations of Demosthenes and Cicero. They are such heavenly sounds as only the twice-born, the true aristocracy of God, can ever utter, "Abba, Father:" they even move the heart of the Eternal.

But it is also very *natural* praying: for a child to say, "Father," is according to the fitness of things. It is not necessary to send your boys to a Board School to teach them to do that. They cry "Father," soon and often. So, when we are born again, "Our Father, which art in heaven," is a prayer that is never forced upon us: it rises up naturally within the new-born nature; and because we are born again we cry, "Abba, Father." When we have lost our Father for awhile, we cry after him in the dark. When he takes the rod to us we cry; but we cry no otherwise than this—"Abba, Father, if it be possible, let this cup pass from me."

It seems to me to be not only an earnest cry and a natural cry, but a very *appealing* cry. It touches your heart when your child says, "Don't hurt me, father. Dear father, by your love to me, forgive me." True prayer pleads the fatherhood of God—"My father, my father, I am no stranger; I am no foe, I am thy own dear and well-beloved child. Therefore, like as a father pitieth his children, have thou pity upon me." The Lord never turns a deaf ear to such pleadings. He says, "I do earnestly remember him still," and in love he checks his hand.

And what a *familiar* word it is—"Abba, Father"! They say that slaves were never allowed to call their masters "abba." That was a word for free-born children only: no man can speak with God as God's children may. I have heard critics say sometimes of our prayers, "How familiar that man is with God"; and one adds, "I do not like such boldness." No, you slaves; of course, you cannot speak with God as a child can; and it would not be right that you should! It befits you to fear, and crouch, and, like miserable sinners, to keep yourselves a long way off from God. Distance is the slave's place; only the child may draw near. But if you are children, then you may say, "Lord, thou hast had mercy upon me, miserable sinner as I was; and thou hast cleansed me, and I am thine; therefore deal with me according to the riches of thy grace. My soul delighteth herself in thee, for thou art my God, and my exceeding joy." Who but a true-born child of God can understand that word—"Delight thyself also in the Lord; and he will give thee the desires of thine heart."

I do not know any more *delightful* expression towards God than to say to him, "Abba, Father." It is as much as to say—"My heart knows that thou art my Father. I am as sure of it as that I am the child of my earthly father; and I am more sure that thou wouldest deal tenderly with me than that my father would." Paul hints at this when he reminds us that our fathers, verily, chastened us after their own pleasure, but the Lord always chastens us for our profit. The heavenly Father's heart is never angry so as to smite in wrath; but in pity, and gentleness, and tenderness, he afflicts his sons and daughters. "Thou in faithfulness hast afflicted me." See what a blessed state this is to be brought into, to be made children of God, and then in our prayers to be praying, not like serfs and servants, but as children who cry, "Abba, Father."

IV. Now, the last thing is, THE SPIRIT OF WITNESS:—"The Spirit itself beareth witness with our spirit, that we are the children of God."

There are two witnesses to the adoption of every child of God. Two is a legal number: in the mouth of two witnesses the whole shall be established. The first witness is *the man's own spirit*. His spirit says, "Yes, yes, yes, I am a child of God. I feel those drawings towards God; I feel that delight in him; I feel that love to him; I feel that wish to obey him, which I never could have felt if I were not his child. Moreover, God's own word declares, 'To as many as received him'—that is Christ—'to them gave he power to become the sons of God, even to them that believe on his name;' now, I have received Christ, and I do believe on his name: therefore, I have the evidence of God's written word that I am one of the sons of God. I have the right, the permission, the authority, to be one of the sons of God. That is the witness of my spirit: I believe, and therefore I am a child."

Now comes in *the witness of the Holy Spirit*. Nobody can question his veracity; but how does the Spirit of God witness to our sonship?

First, he witnesses it, as I have already said, *through the word* of which he is the Author. The word contained in Scripture is quite enough for us if we have a saving faith. We accept it and believe it. The Spirit of God thus witnesses through the Word, and that is the surest medium. "We have a more sure word of testimony," said Peter. That is a wonderful declaration of the apostle. Peter had spoken about seeing Christ transfigured on the holy mount. Was not that sure? Yes, it was but he, in effect, says,—We have a more sure word of testimony than all the sights that we have seen, whereunto we do well if we take heed, as unto a light that shineth in a dark place.

Next, the Spirit of God *bears witness by his work in us*. He works in us that which proves us to be the children of God; and what is that?

The first thing is that he works in us great love to God. None love God but those that are born of him. There is no true love to God in Christ Jesus except in those that have been begotten again by God's own Spirit, so that our love to God is the witness of the Spirit that we are the children of God.

Furthermore, he works in us a veneration for God. We fear before him with a childlike reverence: everything that has to do with God becomes sacred to us when he communes with us. Ay, if he only met us in a dream we should say, "How dreadful is this place! It is none other than the house of God, and it is the very gate of heaven." The place of his feet is glorious in our eyes. The meanest of his chosen are honourable in our esteem. This holy awe of believers is a proof of their being God's children. If he be their Father they will reverence him, for we know that when we had fathers of our flesh, they corrected us, and we gave them reverence, for it was due to them. Shall we not be in subjection to the Father of our spirits? That subjection is the surest evidence that we are indeed the sons of God.

In addition to this, the Spirit of God works in us a holy confidence. By his grace we feel in days of trouble that we can rest in God. When we cannot see our way we go on joyfully without seeing. What is the good of seeing with our own eyes when the eyes of the Lord are running to and fro in the earth to show himself strong in the behalf of all them that trust in him? Our faith feels a joy in believing seeming contradictions, a delight in accepting apparent impossibilities. We have a belief in God's veracity so sure and steadfast that if all the angels in heaven were to deny the truth of God we would laugh them to scorn. *He must be true*, and we know it: every word of his book is as certainly true to us as if we had seen the thing with our own eyes—ay, and truer still, for eyes deceive, and mislead, but God never can. Wherever there is this blessed childlike trust, there is the Spirit's witness that we are the children of God.

And then, again, when the Spirit of God works in us sanctification, that becomes a further witness of our sonship. When he makes us hate sin, when he makes us love everything that is pure and good, when he helps us to conquer ourselves, when he leads us to love our fellowmen, when he fashions us like to Christ, this is the witness of the Spirit with our spirit that we are the children of God. Oh, to have more and more of it!

Besides which, I believe that there is a voice unheard of the outward ear, which drops in silence on the spirit of man, and lets him know that he has, indeed, passed from death unto life. This also is the seal of the Spirit to the truth of our adoption.

Now let us begin at the beginning, and bless him that ever he made us feel the bondage of sin. Let us bless him that he made us fear and tremble, and fly to Jesus. Let us bless him that he has brought us into the adoption of children. Let us bless him that he helps us to cry "Abba, Father"; and, lastly, let us bless him that to-night he bears witness with our spirit that we are the children of God.

Dear friend, dost thou believe in the Lord Jesus Christ? If so, all the privileges of an heir of God are thine. If thou dost not believe in Christ, the Spirit of God will never bear witness to a lie, and tell thee that thou art saved when thou art not. If thou art not saved and not yet a believer in Jesus, I tell thee that thou art like a blank document to which the Spirit of God will never set his hand and seal, for he is never so unwise as to sign a blank. If thou hast believed, thou art a child of God, and the Spirit of God sets his seal to thy adoption. Go in peace, and rejoice in the Lord for ever.

> Nor fret, nor doubt, nor suffer slavish fear:
> Thy spirit is released, thy path is clear.
> Let praise fill up thy day, and evermore
> Live thou to love, to copy, and adore.

4

THE POWER OF THE HOLY GHOST

"The power of the Holy Ghost,"—Rom. 15:13.

~

POWER is the special and peculiar prerogative of God, and God alone. "Twice have I have heard this: that power belongeth unto God" God is God: and power belongeth to him. If he delegates a portion of it to his creatures, yet still it is *his* power. The sun, although he is "like a bridegroom coming out of his chamber, and rejoiceth as a strong man to run his race," yet has no power to perform his motions except as God directs him. The stars, although they travel in their orbits and none could stay them, yet have neither might nor force except that which God daily infuses into them. The tall archangel, near his throne, who outshines a comet in its blaze, though he is one of those who excel in strength and hearken to the voice of the commands of God, yet has no might except that which his Maker gives to him. As for Leviathan, who so maketh the sea to boil like a pot that one would think the deep were hoary: as for Behemoth, who drinketh up Jordan at a draught, and boasteth that he can snuff up rivers; as for those majestic creatures that are found on earth, they owe their strength to him who fashioned their bones of steel and made their sinews of brass. And when we think of man if he has might or power, it is so small and insignificant, that we can scarcely call it such; yea, when it is at its greatest—when he sways his sceptre, when he commands hosts, when he rules nations—still the power belongeth unto God; and it is true, "Twice have I heard this, that power belongeth unto God." This exclusive prerogative, of God, is to be found in each of the three persons of the glorious Trinity. The Father hath power: for by his word were the heavens made, and all the host of them; by his strength all things stand, and through him they fulfil their destiny. The Son hath power: for like his Father, he is the Creator of all things; "Without him was not anything made that was made," and "by him all things consist." And the Holy Spirit hath power. It is concerning the power of the Holy Ghost that I shall speak this morning; and may you have a practical exemplification of that attribute in your own hearts, when you shall feel that the influence of the Holy Ghost is being poured out upon me, so that I am speaking the words of the living God to your souls, and bestowed upon you when you are feeling the effects of it in your own spirits.

We shall look at the power of the Holy Ghost in three ways this morning. First, *the outward and visible displays of it*; second, *the inward and spiritual manifestations of: it* and third, *the future and expected works thereof*. The power of the Spirit will thus I trust, be made clearly present to your souls.

I. First, then, we are to view the power of the Spirit in the OUTWARD AND VISIBLE DISPLAYS OF IT. The power of the Spirit has not been dormant; it has exerted itself. Much has been done by the spirit of God already: more than could have been accomplished by any being except the Infinite, Eternal, Almighty Jehovah, of whom the Holy Spirit is one person. There are four works which are the outward and manifest signs of the power of the Spirit: creation works: resurrection works: works of attestation, or of witness: and works of grace. Of each of the works I shall speak very briefly.

1. First, the Spirit has manifested the omnipotence of his power in *creation works*: for though not very frequently in Scripture, yet sometimes creation is ascribed to the Holy Ghost, as well as to the Father and the Son. The creation of the heavens above us is said to be the work of God's Spirit. This you will see at once by referring to the sacred Scriptures, Job 26, 13th verse, "By his Spirit he hath garnished the heavens; his hand hath formed the crooked serpent." All the stars of heaven are said to have been placed aloft by the Spirit, and one particular constellation called the "crooked serpent" is specially pointed out as his handiwork. He looseth the bands of Orion; he bindeth the sweet influences of the Pleiades, and guides Acturus with his sons. He made all those stars that shine in heaven. The heavens were garnished by his hands, and he formed the crooked serpent by his might. So also in those continued acts of creation which are still performed in the world; as the bringing forth of man and animals, their birth and generation. These are ascribed also to the Holy Ghost. If you look at the 104th Psalm, at the 29th verse, you will read, "Thou hidest thy face, they are troubled: thou takest away their breath, they die, and return to their dust. Thou sendest forth thy Spirit, they are created: and thou renewest the face of the earth." So that the creation of every man is the work of the Spirit: and the creation of all life and all flesh-existence in this world is as much to be ascribed to the power of the Spirit as the first garnishing of the heavens, or the fashioning of the crooked serpent. But if you will look in the 1st chapter of Genesis, you will there see more particularly set forth that peculiar operation of power upon the universe which was put forth by the Holy Spirit; you will then discover what was his special work. In the 2nd verse of the 1st chapter of Genesis, we read, "And the earth was without form, and void; and darkness was upon the face of the deep. And the Spirit of God moved upon the face of the waters." We know not how remote

the period of the creation of this globe may be—certainly many millions of years before the time of Adam. Our planet has passed through various stages of existence, and different kinds of creatures have lived on its surface, all of which have been fashioned by God. But before that era came, wherein man should be its principal tenant and monarch, the Creator gave up the world to confusion. He allowed the inward fires to burst up from beneath and melt all the solid matter, so that all kinds of substances were commingled in one vast mass of dissorder; the only name you could give to the world then was, that it was a chaotic mass of matter; what it should be, you could not guess or define. It was entirely without form, and void; and darkness was upon the face of the deep. The Spirit came, and stretching his broad wings, bade the darkness disperse, and as he moved over it, all the different portions of matter came into their places, and it was no longer "without form, and void;" but became round like its sister planets, and moved, singing the high praises of God—not discordantly as it had done before, but as one great note in the vast scale of creation. Milton very beautifully describes this work of the Spirit in thus bringing order out confusion, when the King of Glory, in his powerful Word and Spirit, came to create new worlds:—

> "On heavenly ground they stood; and from the shore
> They view'd the vast immeasurable abyss
> Outrageous as a sea, dark, wasteful, wild,
> Up from the bottom turn'd by furious winds
> And surging waves, as mountains, to assault
> Heaven's height, and with the centre mix the pole.
>
> "Silence ye troubled waves, and thou deep, peace,
> Said then the Omnific Word; your discord end.
>   Then on the watery calm
> His brooding wings the Spirit of God outspread
> And vital virtue infused, and vital warmth
> Throughout the fluid mass."

This you see then is the power of the Spirit. Could we have seen that earth all in confusion, we should have said, "Who can make a world out of this?" The answer would have been, "The power of the Spirit can do it. By the simple spreading of his dove-like wings he can make all the things come together. Upon that there shall be order where there was nought but confusion." Nor is this all the power of the Spirit. We have seen some of his works in creation. But there was one particular instance of creation in which the Holy Spirit was more especially concerned; viz., the formation of the body of our Lord Jesus Christ. Though our Lord Jesus Christ was born of a woman and made in the likeness of sinful flesh, yet the power that begat him was entirely in God the Holy Spirit—as the Scriptures, express it, "The power of the Highest shall overshadow thee." He was begotten as the Apostles' Creed says, begotten of the Holy Ghost. "That holy thing which is born of thee shall be called the Son of the Highest." The corporeal frame of the Lord Jesus Christ was a masterpiece of the Holy Spirit. I suppose his body to have excelled all others in beauty; to have been like that of the first man, the very pattern of what the body is to be in heaven, when it shall shine forth in all its glory. That fabric, in all its beauty and perfection, was modelled by the Spirit. In his book were all the members written when as yet there were none of them. He fashioned and formed him; and here again we have another instance of the creative energy of the Spirit.

2. A second manifestation of the Holy Spirit's power is to be found in the *resurrection of the Lord Jesus Christ*. If ye have ever studied this subject, ye have perhaps been rather perplexed to find that sometimes the resurrection of Christ is ascribed to himself. By his own power and Godhead he could not be held by the bond of death, but as he willingly gave up his life he had power to take it again. In another portion of Scripture you find it ascribed to God the Father: "He raised him up from the dead:" "Him hath

God the Father exalted." And many other passages of similar import. But, again, it is said in Scripture that Jesus Christ was raised by the Holy Spirit. Now all these things were true. He was raised by the Father because the Father said, "Loose the prisoner—let him go. Justice is satisfied. My law requires no more satisfaction—vengeance has had its due—let him go." Here he gave an official message which delivered Jesus from the grave. He was raised by his own majesty and power because he had a right to come out; and he felt he had and therefore "burst the bonds of death: he could be no longer holden of them." But he was raised by the Spirit as to that energy which his mortal frame received, by the which it rose again from the grave after having lain there for three days and nights. If you want proofs of this you must open your Bibles again, 1 Peter, 3:18. "For Christ also hath once suffered for sins, the just for the unjust, that he might bring us to God, being put to death in the flesh but quickened by the Spirit." And a further proof you may find in Romans, 8:11.—(I love sometimes to be textual, for I believe the great fault of Christians is that they do not search the Scriptures enough, and I will make them search them when they are here if they do not do so anywhere else.)— "But if the Spirit of him that raised up Jesus from the dead dwell in you, he that raised up Christ from the dead shall also quicken your mortal bodies by his Spirit that dwelleth in you."

The resurrection of Christ, then, was effected by the agency of the Spirit; and here we have a noble illustration of his omnipotence. Could you have stepped, as angels did, into the grave of Jesus, and seen his sleeping body, you would have found it cold as any other corpse. Lift up the hand; it falls by the side. Look at the eye: it is glazed. And there is a death-thrust which must have annihilated life. See his hands: the blood distils not from them. They are cold and motionless. Can that body live? Can it start up? Yes; and be and illustration of the might of the Spirit. For when the power of the Spirit came on him, as it was when it fell upon the dry bones of the valley: "he arose in the majesty of his divinity, and bright and shining, astonished the watchmen so that they fled away; yea, he arose no more to die, but to live for ever, King of kings and Prince of the kings of the earth."

3. The third of the works of the Holy Spirit which have so wonderfully demonstrated his power, are *attestation works*. I mean by this,—works of witnessing. When Jesus Christ went into the stream of baptism in the river Jordan, the Holy Spirit descended upon him like a dove, and proclaimed him God's beloved son. That was what I style an attestation work. And when afterwards Jesus Christ raised the dead, when he healed the leper, when he spoke to diseases and they fled apace, when demons rushed in thousands from those who were possessed of them, it was done by the power of the Spirit. The Spirit dwelt in Jesus without measure, and by that power all those miracles were worked. These were attestation works. And when Jesus Christ was gone, you will remember that master attestation of the Spirit when he came like a rushing mighty wind upon the assembled apostles, and cloven tongues sat upon them; and you will remember how he attested their ministry by giving them to speak with tongues as he gave them utterance; and how, also, miraculous deeds were wrought by them, how they taught, how Peter raised Dorcas, how he breathed life into Eutycus, how great deeds were wrought by the apostles as well as their Master—so that "mighty signs and wonders were done by the Holy Ghost, and many believed thereby." Who will doubt the power of the Holy Spirit after that? Ah! those Socinians who deny the existence of the Holy Ghost and his absolute personality, what will they do when we get them on creation, resurrection, and attestation? They must rush in the very teeth of Scripture. But mark! it is a stone upon which if any man fall he shall be bruised; but if it fall upon him, as it will do if he resists it, it shall grind him to

powder. The Holy Spirit has power omnipotent, even the power of God.

4. Once more, if we want another outward and visible sign of the power of the Spirit, we may look at the *works of grace*. Behold a city where a soothsayer hath the power—who has given out himself to be some great one, a Philip enters it and preaches the Word of God, straightway a Simon Magus loses his power and himself seeks for the power of the Spirit to be given to him, fancying it might be purchased with money. See, in modern times, a country where the inhabitants live in miserable wigwams, feeding on reptiles and the meanest creatures; observe them bowing down before their idols and worshipping their false gods, and so plunged in superstition, so degraded and debased, that it became a question whether they had souls or not; behold a Moffat go with the Word of God in his hand, hear him preach as the Spirit gives him utterance, and accompanies that Word with power. They cast aside their idols—they hate and abhor their former lusts; they build houses, wherein they dwell; they become clothed, and in their right mind. They break the bow, and cut the spear in sunder; the uncivilized become civilized; the savage becomes polite; he who knew nothing begins to read the Scriptures; thus out of the mouths of Hottentots God attests the power of his mighty Spirit. Take a household in this city—and we could guide you to many such—the father is a drunkard; he has been the most desperate of characters; see him in his madness, and you might just as well meet an unchained tiger as meet such a man. He seems as if he could rend a man to pieces who should offend him. Mark his wife. She, too, has a spirit in her, and when he treats her ill she can resist him; many broils have been seen in that house, and often has the neighbourhood been disturbed by the noise created there. As for the poor little children—see them in their rags and nakedness, poor untaught things. Untaught, did I say? They are taught and well taught in the devil's school, and

are growing up to be the heirs of damnation. But some one whom God has blessed by his Spirit is guided to the house. He may be but a humble city missionary perhaps, but he speaks to such a one: O, says he, come and listen to the voice of God. Whether it is by his own agency, or a minister's preaching, the Word, which is quick and powerful, cuts to the sinner's heart. The tears run down his cheeks—such as had never been seen before. He shakes and quivers. The strong man bows down—the mighty man trembles—and those knees that never shook begin to knock together. That heart which never quailed before, now begins to shake before the power of the Spirit. He sits down on a humble bench by the penitent; he lets his knees bend, whilst his lips utter a child's prayer, but, whilst a child's prayer, a prayer of a child of God. He becomes a changed character. Mark the reformation in his house! That wife of his becomes the decent matron. Those children are the credit of the house, and in due time they grow up like olive branches round his table, adorning his house like polished stones. Pass by the house—no noise or broils, but songs of Zion. See him—no drunken revelry; he has drained his last cup; and, now forswearing it, he comes to God and is his servant. Now, you will not hear at midnight the bacchanalian shout; but should there be a noise, it will be the sound of the solemn hymn of praise to God. And, now, is there not such a thing as the power of the Spirit? Yes! and these must have witnessed it, and seen it I know a village, once, perhaps, the most profane in England—a village inundated by drunkenness and debauchery of the worst kind, where it was impossible almost for an honest traveller to stop in the public house without being annoyed by blasphemy; a place noted for incendiaries and robbers. One man, the ringleader of all, listened to the voice of God. That man's heart was broken. The whole gang came to hear the gospel preached, and they sat and seemed to reverence the preacher as if he were a God, and not a man. These men became changed and reformed; and every one who knows the place affirms that such a change had never been wrought but by the power of the Holy Ghost. Let the gospel be preached and the Spirit poured out, and you will see that it has such power to change the conscience, to ameliorate the conduct, to raise the debased, to chastise and to curb the wickedness of the race, that you must glory in it. I say, there is nought like the power of the Spirit. Only let that come, and, indeed, everything can be accomplished.

II. Now, for the second point, THE INWARD AND SPIRITUAL POWER OF THE HOLY SPIRIT. What I have already spoken of may be seen; what I am about to speak of must be felt, and no man will apprehend what I say with truth unless he has felt it. The other, even the infidel must confess; the other, the greatest blasphemer cannot deny it he speaks the truth; but this is what the one will laugh at as enthusiasm and what the other will say is but the invention of our fevered fancies. However, we have a more sure word of testimony than all that they may say. We have a witness within. We know it is the truth, and we are not afraid to speak of the inward spiritual power of the Holy Ghost. Let us notice two or three things wherein the inward and spiritual power of the Holy Ghost is very greatly to be seen and extolled.

1. First, in that the Holy Ghost has *a power over men's hearts*. Now, men's hearts are very hard to affect. If you want to get at them for any worldly object you can do it. A cheating world can win man's heart; a little gold can win man's heart; a trump of fame and a little clamour of applause can win man's heart. But there is not a minister breathing that can win man's heart himself. He can win his ears and make them listen; he can win his eyes, and fix those eyes upon him; he can win the attention, but the heart is very slippery. Yes, the heart is a fish that troubles all gospel fishermen to hold. You may sometimes pull it almost all out of the water; but slimy as an eel, it slippeth between your fingers, and you have not captured it after

all. Many a man has fancied that he has caught the heart but has been disappointed. It would need a strong hunter to overtake the hart on the mountains. It is too fleet for human foot to approach. The Spirit alone has power over man's heart. Do you ever try your power on a heart? If any man thinks that a minister can convert the soul, I wish he would try. Let him go and be a Sabbath-school teacher. He shall take his class, he shall have the best books that can be obtained, he shall have the best rules, he shall draw his lines of circumvallation about his spiritual Sebastopol, he shall take the best boy in his class, and if he is not tired in a week I shall be very much mistaken. Let him spend four or five Sabbaths in trying, but he will say, "The young fellow is incorrigible." Let him try another. And he will have to try another, and another, and another, before he will manage to convert one. He will soon find "It is not by might nor by power, but by my Spirit, saith the Lord." Can a minister convert? Can he touch the heart? David said, "Your hearts are as fat as grease." Ay, that is quite true; and we cannot get through so much grease at all. Our sword cannot get at the heart, it is encased in so much fatness; it is harder than a nether millstone. Many a good old Jerusalem blade has been blunted against the hard heart. Many a piece of the true steel that God has put into the hands of his servants has had the edge turned by being set up against the sinner's heart. We cannot reach the soul; but the Holy Spirit can. "My beloved can put in his hand by the hole in the door and my bowels will move for sin." He can give a sense of blood-bought pardon that shall dissolve a heart of stone. He can

> "Speak with that voice which wakes the dead,
>   And bids the sinner rise:
> And makes the guilty conscience dread
>   The death that never dies."

He can make Sinai's thunders audible; yea, and he can make the sweet whisperings of Calvary enter into the soul.

He has power over the heart of man. And here is a glorious proof of the omnipotence of the Spirit that he has rule over the heart.

2. But if there is one thing more stubborn than the heart it is *the will*. "My lord Will-be-will," as Bunyan calls him in his "Holy War," is a fellow who will not easily be bent. The will, especially in some men, is a very stubborn thing, and in all men, if the will is once stirred up to opposition, there is nothing can be done with them. *Freewill* somebody believes in. *Freewill* many dream of. Freewill! wherever is that to be found? Once there was free will in Paradise, and a terrible mess free will made there, for it all spoiled all Paradise and turned Adam out of the garden. Free will was once in heaven; but it turned the glorious archangel out, and a third part of the stars of heaven fell into the abyss. I want nothing to do with free will, but I will try to see whether I have got a free will within. And I find I have. Very free will to evil, but very poor will to that which is good. Free will enough when I sin, but when I would do good evil is present with me, and how to do that which I would I find not. Yet some boast of free will. I wonder whether those who believe in it have any more power over persons wills than I have. I know I have not any. I find the old proverb very true, "One man can bring a horse to the water, but a hundred cannot make him drink." I find that I can bring you all to the water, and a great many more than can get into this chapel; but I cannot make you drink; and I don't think a hundred ministers could make you drink. I have read old Rowland Hill, and Whitfield, and several others, to see what they did; but I cannot discover a plan of turning your wills. I cannot coax you; and you will not yield by any manner of means. I do not think any man has power over his fellow-creature's will, but the Spirit of God has. "I will make them willing in the day of my power." He maketh the unwilling sinner so willing that he is impetuous after the gospel; he who was obstinate, now hurries to the cross. He

who laughed at Jesus, now hangs on his mercy; and he who would not believe, is now made by the Holy Spirit to do it, not only willingly, but eagerly; he is happy, is glad to do it, rejoices in the sound of Jesus' name, and delights to run in the way of God's commandments. The Holy Spirit has power over the will.

3. And yet there is one thing more which I think is rather worse than the will. You will guess what I mean. The will is somewhat worse than the heart to bend, but there is one thing that excels the will in its naughtiness, and that is the *imagination*. I hope that my will is managed by Divine Grace. But I am afraid my imagination is not at times. Those who have a fair share of imagination know what a difficult thing it is to control. You cannot restrain it. It will break the reins. You will never be able to manage it. The imagination will sometimes fly up to God with such a power that eagles' wings cannot match it. It sometimes has such might that it can almost see the King in his beauty, and the land which is very far off. With regard to myself, my imagination will sometimes take me over the gates of iron, across that infinite unknown, to the very gates of pearl, and discovers the blessed glorified. But if it is potent one way it is another; for my imagination has taken me down to the vilest kennels and sewers of earth. It has given me thoughts so dreadful, that while I could not avoid them, yet I was thoroughly horrified at them. These thoughts will come; and when I feel in the holiest frame, the most devoted to God, and the most earnest in prayer, it often happens that that is the very time when the plagues breaks out the worst. But I rejoice and think of one thing, that I can cry out when this imagination comes upon me. I know it is said in the Book of Leviticus, when an act of evil was committed, if the maiden cried out against it, then her life was to be spared. So it is with the Christian. If he cries out, there is hope. Can you chain your imagination? No; but the power of the Holy Ghost can. Ah, it shall do it, and it does do it at last; it does it even on earth.

III. But the last thing was, THE FUTURE AND DESIRED EFFECTS; for after all, though the Holy Spirit has done so much, he cannot say, "It is finished." Jesus Christ could exclaim concerning his own labor—"It is finished." But the Holy Spirit cannot say that. He has more to do yet: and until the consummation of all things, when the Son himself becomes subject to the Father, it shall not be said by the Holy Spirit, "It is finished." What, then, has the Holy Spirit to do?

1. First, he has to *perfect us in holiness*. There are two kinds of perfection which a Christian needs—one is the perfection of justification in the person of Jesus; and the other is, the perfection of sanctification worked in him by the Holy Spirit. At present corruption still rests even in the breasts of the regenerate. At present the heart is partially impure. At present there are still lusts and evil imaginations. But, Oh! my soul rejoices to know that the day is coming when God shall finish the work which he has begun; and he shall present my soul, not only perfect in Christ, but, perfect in the Spirit, without spot or blemish, or any such thing. And is it true that this poor depraved heart is to become as holy as that of God? And is it true that this poor spirit, which often cries, "O wretched man that I am, who shall deliver me from the body of this sin and death!" shall get rid of sin and death—I shall have no evil things to vex my ears, and no unholy thoughts to disturb my peace? Oh! happy hour! may it be hastened! Just before I die, sanctification will be finished; but not till that moment shall I ever claim perfection in myself. But at that moment when I depart, my spirit shall have its last baptism in the Holy Spirit's fire. It shall be put in the crucible for its last trying in the furnace; and then, free from all dross, and fine like a wedge of pure gold, it shall be presented at the feet of God without the least degree of dross or mixture. O glorious hour! O blessed moment! Methinks I long to die if there were no heaven, if I might but have that last purification,

and come up from Jordan's stream most white from the washing. Oh! to be washed white, clean, pure, perfect! Not an angel more pure than I shall be—yea, not God himself more holy! And I shall be able to say, in a double sense, "Great God, I am clean—through Jesus's blood I am clean, through the Spirit's work I am clean too!" Must we not extol the power of the Holy Ghost in thus making us fit to stand before our Father in heaven?

2. Another great work of the Holy Spirit which is not accomplished is *the bringing on of the latter-day glory*. In a few more years—I know not when, I know not how—the Holy Spirit will be poured out in a far different style from the present. There are diversities of operations; and during the last few years it has been the case that the diversified operations have consisted in very little pouring out of the Spirit. Ministers have gone on in dull routine, continually preaching—preaching—preaching, and little good has been done. I do hope that perhaps a fresh era has dawned upon us, and that there is a better pouring out of the Spirit even now. For the hour is coming, and it may be even now is, when the Holy Ghost shall be poured out again in such a wonderful manner that many shall run to and fro, and knowledge shall be increased—the knowledge of the Lord shall cover the earth as the waters cover the surface of the great deep; when his kingdom shall come, and his will shall be done on earth even as it is in heaven. We are not going to be dragging on for ever like Pharoah with the wheels off his chariot. My heart exults and my eyes flash with the thought that very likely I shall live to see the out-pouring of the Spirit; when "the sons and the daughters of God again shall prophecy, and the young men shall see visions, and the old men shall dream dreams." Perhaps there shall be no miraculous gifts—for they will not be required; but yet there shall be such a miraculous amount of holiness, such an extraordinary fervour of prayer, such a real communion with God and so much vital religion, and such a spread of the doctrines of the cross, that every one will

see that verily the Spirit is poured out like water, and the rains are descending from above. For that let us pray: let us continually labor for it, and seek it of God.

3. One more work of the Spirit which will especially manifest his power—*the general resurrection*. We have reason to believe from Scripture that the resurrection of the dead, whilst it will be effected by the voice of God and of his Word, (the Son) shall also be brought about by the Spirit. That same power which raised Jesus Christ from the dead, shall also quicken your mortal bodies. The power of the resurrection is perhaps one of the finest proofs of the works of the Spirit. Ah! my friends, if this earth could but have its mantle torn away for a little while, if the green sod could be cut from it, and we could look about six feet deep into its bowels, what a world it would seem! What should we see? Bones, carcasses, rottenness, worms, corruption. And you would say, "Can these dry bones live? Can they start up?" "Yes! in a moment! in the twinkling of an eye, at the last trump, the dead shall be raised." He speaks: they are alive! See them scattered: bone comes to his bone! See them naked: flesh comes upon them! See them still lifeless: "Come from the four winds, O breath, and breathe upon these slain!" When the wind of the Holy Spirit comes, they live, and they stand upon their feet an exceeding great army.

I have thus attempted to speak of the power of the Spirit, and I trust I have shewn it to you. We must now have a moment or two for practical inference. The Spirit is very powerful, Christian! what do you infer from that fact? Why, that you never need distrust the power of God to carry you to heaven. O how that sweet verse was laid to my soul yesterday!

> "His tried Almighty arm
>   Is raised for your defence;
> Where is the power can reach you there?
>   Or what can pluck you thence?"

The power of the Holy Spirit is your bulwark, and all his omnipotence defends you. Can your enemies overcome omnipotence? then they can conquer you. Can they wrestle with Diety, and hurl him to the ground? then they might conquer you. For the power of the Spirit is our power; the power of the Spirit is our might.

Once again, Christians, if this is the power of the Spirit, *why should you doubt anything*? There is your son. There is that wife of yours for whom you have supplicated so frequently: do not doubt the Spirit's power. "Though he tarry, wait for him." There is thy husband, O holy woman! and thou hast wrestled for his soul. And though he is ever so hardened and desperate a wretch, and treats thee ill, there is power in the Spirit. And, O ye who have come from barren churches with scarcely a leaf upon the tree. Do not doubt the power of the Spirit to raise you up. For it shall be a "pasture for flocks, a den of wild asses," open, but deserted, until the Spirit is poured out from on high. And then the parched ground shall be made a pool, and the thirsty land springs of water, and in the habitations of dragons, where each lay shall be grass with reeds and rushes. And, O ye members of Park Street! ye who remember what your God has done for you especially, never distrust the power of the Spirit. Ye have seen the wilderness blossom like Carmel, ye have seen the desert blossom like the rose; trust him for the future. Then go out and labour with this conviction, that the power of the Holy Ghost is able to do anything. Go to your Sunday-school; go to your tract distribution; go to your missionary enterprise! go to your preaching in your rooms, with the conviction that the power of the Spirit is our great help.

And now, lastly to you sinners:—What is there to be said to you about this power of the Spirit? Why, to me, there is some hope for some of you. I cannot save you: I cannot get at you. I make you cry sometimes—you wipe your eyes, and it is all over. But I know my Master can. That is my consolation. Chief of sinners, there is hope for thee! This power can save you as well as anybody else. It is able to break your heart, though it is an iron one; to make your eyes run with tears though they have been like rocks before. His power is able this morning, if he will, to change your heart, to turn the current of all your ideas; to make you at once a child of God, to justify you in Christ. There is power enough in the Holy Spirit. Ye are not straightened in him, but in your own bowels. He is able to bring sinners to Jesus: he is able to make you willing in the day of his power. Are you willing this morning? Has he gone so far as to make you desire his name, to make you wish for Jesus? Then, O sinner! whilst he draws you, say, "Draw me, I am wretched without thee." Follow him, follow him; and, while he leads, tread you in his footsteps, and rejoice that he has begun a good work in you, for there is an evidence that he will continue it even unto the end. And, O desponding one! put thy trust in the power of the Spirit. Rest on the blood of Jesus, and thy soul is safe, not only now, but throughout eternity. God bless you, my hearers. Amen.

5
THE COMFORTER

"But the Comforter, which is the Holy Ghost, whom the Father will send in my name, he shall teach you all things, and bring all things to your remembrance, whatsoever I have said unto you."—John 14:26.

~

GOOD old Simeon called Jesus the consolation of Israel: and so he was. Before his actual appearance, his name was the Day-Star; cheering the darkness, and prophetic of the rising sun. To him they looked with the same hope which cheers the nightly watcher, when from the lonely castle-top he sees the fairest of the stars, and hails her as the usher of the morn. When he was on earth, he must have been the consolation of all those who were privileged to be his companions. We can imagine how readily the disciples would run to Christ to tell him of their griefs, and how sweetly with that matchless intonation of his voice, he would speak to them and bid their fears be gone. Like children, they would consider him as their Father; and to him every want, every groan, every sorrow, every agony, would at once be carried; and he, like a wise physician, had a balm for every wound; he had mingled a cordial for their every care; and readily did he dispense some mighty remedy to allay all the fever of their troubles. Oh! it must have been sweet to have lived with Christ. Surely sorrows then were but joys in masks, because they gave an opportunity to go to Jesus to have them removed. Oh! would to God, some of us may say, that we could have lain our weary heads upon the bosom of Jesus, and that our birth had been in that happy era, when we might have heard his kind voice, and seen his kind look, when he said "Let the weary ones come unto me."

But now he was about to die. Great prophecies were to be fulfilled, and great purposes were to be answered and therefore Jesus must go. It behoved him to suffer, that he might be made a propitiation for our sins. It behoved him to slumber in the dust awhile, that he might perfume the chamber of the grave to make it—

"No more a charnel house to fence
The relics of lost innocence."

It behoved him to have a resurrection, that we who shall one day be the dead in Christ, might rise first, and in glorious bodies stand upon earth. And it behoved him that he should ascend up on high, that he might lead captivity captive; that he might chain the fiends of hell; that he might lash them to his chariot wheels and drag them up high heaven's hill, to make them feel a second overthrow from his right arm when he should dash them from the pinnacles of heaven down to deeper depths beneath. "It is right I should go away from you," said Jesus, "for if I go not away, the Comforter will not come." Jesus must go. Weep ye disciples. Jesus must be gone. Mourn ye poor ones who are to be left without a Comforter. But hear how kindly Jesus speaks: "I will not leave you comfortless, I will pray the Father, and he shall send you another Comforter, who shall be with you, and shall dwell in you forever." He would not leave those few poor sheep alone in the wilderness; he would not desert his children and leave them fatherless. Albeit that he had a mighty mission which did fill his heart and hand; albeit that he had so much to perform that we might have thought that even his gigantic intellect would be overburdened; albeit he had so much to suffer, that we might suppose his whole soul to be concentrated upon the thought of the sufferings to be endured; yet it was not so; before he left, he gave soothing words of comfort; like the good Samaritan, he poured in oil and wine; and we see what he promised: "I will send you another Comforter—one who shall be just what I have been, yea even more; who shall console you in your sorrows, remove your doubts, comfort you in your afflictions, and stand as my vicar on earth, to do that which I would have done, had I tarried with you."

Before I discourse of the Holy Ghost as the Comforter, I must make one or two remarks on the different translations of the word rendered "Comforter." The Rhemish translation, which you are aware is adopted by Roman Catholics, has left the word untranslated, and gives it "Paraclete." "But the Paraclete which is the Holy Ghost, whom the Father will send in my name, he shall teach you all things." This is the original Greek word, and it has some other meanings besides "Comforter." Sometimes it means the monitor or instructor: "I will send you another monitor, another teacher." Frequently it means "Advocate;" but the most common meaning of the word is that which we have here: "I will send you another *Comforter*." However, we cannot pass over those other two interpretations without saying something upon them.

"I will send you another *teacher*." Jesus Christ had been the official teacher or his saints whilst on earth. They called no man Rabbi except Christ. They sat at no men's feet to learn their doctrines; but they had them direct from the lips of him who "spake as never man spake." "And now," says he, "when I am gone, where shall you find the great infallible teacher? Shall I set you up a Pope at Rome, to whom you shall go, and who shall be your infallible oracle? Shall I give you the councils of the church to be held to decide all knotty points?" Christ said no such thing.

"I am the infallible paraclete or teacher, and when I am gone, I will send you another teacher and he shall be the person who is to explain Scripture; he shall be the authoritative oracle of God, who shall make all dark things light, who shall unravel mysteries, who shall unravel mysteries, who shall untwist all knots of revelation, and shall make you understand what you could not discover, had it not been for his influence." And beloved, no man ever learns anything aright, unless he is taught of the Spirit. You may learn election, and you may know it so that you shall be damned by it, if you are not taught of the Holy Ghost; for I have known some who have learned election to their soul's destruction; they have learned it, so that they said they were of the elect, whereas they had no marks, no evidences and no work of the Holy Ghost in their souls. There is a way of learning truth in Satan's college, and holding it in licentiousness; but if so, it shall be to your souls as poison to your veins, and prove your everlasting ruin. No man can know Jesus Christ unless he is taught of God. There is no doctrine of the Bible which can be safely, thoroughly, and truly learned, except by the agency of the one authoritative teacher. Ah! tell me not of systems of divinity; tell me not of schemes of theology; tell me not of infallible commentators, or most learned and most arrogant doctors; but tell me of the Great Teacher, who shall instruct us, the sons of God, and shall make us wise to understand all things. He is *the* Teacher: it matters not what this or that man says; I rest on no man's boasting authority, nor will you. Ye are not to be carried away with the craftiness of men, nor sleight of words; this is the authoritative oracle, the Holy Ghost resting in the hearts of his children.

The other translation is *advocate*. Have you ever thought how the Holy Ghost can be said to be an advocate? You know Jesus Christ is called the wonderful, the counsellor, and mighty God; but how can the Holy Ghost be said to be an advocate? I suppose it is thus: he is an advocate on earth to plead against the enemies of the cross. How was it that Paul could so ably plead before Felix and Agrippa? How was it that the Apostles stood unawed before the magistrates and confessed their Lord? How has it come to pass that in all times God's ministers have been made fearless as lions, and their brows have been firmer than brass, their hearts sterner than steel, and their words like the language of God? Why, it is simply for this reason, that it was not the man who pleaded, but it was God the Holy Ghost pleading through him. Have you never seen an earnest minister, with hands uplifted and eyes dropping tears, pleading with the sons of men? Have you never admired that portrait from the hand of old John Bunyan? A grave person with eyes uplifted to heaven, the best of books in his hand, the law of truth written on his lips, the world behind his back, standing as if he pleaded with men, and a crown of gold hanging over his head. Who gave that minister so blessed a manner and such goodly matter? Whence came his skill? Did he acquire it in the college? Did he learn it in the seminary? Ah! no; he learned it of the God of Jacob; he learned it of the Holy Ghost; for the Holy Ghost is the great counsellor who teaches us how to advocate his cause aright.

But, besides this, the Holy Ghost is the advocate in men's hearts. Ah! I have known men reject a doctrine until the Holy Ghost began to illumine them. We who are the advocates of the truth are often very poor pleaders; we spoil our cause by the words we use; but it is a mercy that the brief is in the hand of a special pleader, who will advocate successfully and overcome the sinner's opposition. Did you ever know him fail once? Brethen, I speak to your souls has not God in old times convinced you of sin? Did not the Holy Ghost come and prove that you were guilty, although no minister could ever get you out of your self-righteousness? Did he not advocate Christ's righteousness? Did he not stand and tell you that your works were filthy rags? and when you had well-nigh still refused to listen to his voice, did he not fetch hell's drum and make it sound about your ears, bidding you look through the vista of future years and see the throne set, and the books open, and the sword brandished, and hell burning, and fiends howling, and the damned shrieking forever? And did he not convince you of the judgment to come? He is a mighty advocate when he pleads in the soul—of sin, of righteousness, and of the judgment to come. Blessed advocate! plead in my heart, plead with my conscience. When I sin, make conscience bold to tell me of it; when I err, make conscience speak at once; and when I turn aside to crooked ways, then advocate the cause of righteousness, and bid me sit down in confusion, knowing my guiltiness in the sight of God.

But there is yet another sense in which the Holy Ghost advocates, and that is, he advocates our cause with Jesus Christ, with groanings that cannot be uttered. O my soul, thou art ready to burst within me! O my heart, thou art swelled with grief; the hot tide of my emotion would well-nigh overflow the channels of my veins. I long to speak, but the very desire chains my tongue. I wish to pray, but the fervency of my feeling curbs my language. There is a groaning within that cannot be uttered. Do you know who can utter that groaning, who can understand it, and who can put it into heavenly language and utter it in a celestial tongue, so that Christ can hear it? Oh! yes; it is God the Holy Spirit; he advocates our cause with Christ, and then Christ advocates it with his Father. He is the advocate, who maketh intercession for us, with groanings that cannot be uttered.

Having thus explained the Spirit's office as teacher and advocate, we come now to the translation of our version—the *Comforter*; and here I shall have three divisions. First, the *comforter*; secondly, the *comfort*; and thirdly, the *comforted*.

I. First, then, the COMFORTER. Briefly let me run over in my mind and in your minds too, the characteristics of this glorious Comforter. Let me tell you some of the attributes of his comfort, so that you may understand how well adapted he is to your case.

And first, we will remark that God the Holy Ghost is a very *loving* Comforter. I am in distress and want consolation. Some passer-by hears of my sorrow, and he steps within, sits down and essays to cheer me; he speaks soothing words; but he loves me not, he is a stranger, he knows me not at all, he has only come in to try his skill; and what is the consequence? his words run oe'r me like oil upon a slab of marble—they are like the pattering rain upon the rock; they do not break my grief; it stands unmoved as adamant, because he has no love for me. But let some one who loves me dearly as his own life come and plead with me, then truly his words are music; they taste like honey; he knows the pass-word of the doors of my heart, and my ear is attentive to every word; I catch the intonation of each syllable as it falls, for it is like the harmony of the harps of heaven. Oh! there is a voice in love, it speaks a language which is its own, it is a idiom and an accent which none can mimic; wisdom cannot imitate it; oratory cannot attain unto it; it is love alone which can reach the mourning heart; love is the only handkerchief which can wipe the mourner's tears away. And is not the Holy Ghost a loving Comforter? Dost thou know, O saint, how much the Holy Spirit loves thee? Canst thou measure the love of the Spirit. Dost thou know how great is the affection of his soul towards thee? Go, measure heaven with thy span; go, weigh the mountains in the scales; go, take the ocean's water, and tell each drop; go, count the sand upon the sea's wide shore; and when thou hast accomplished this, thou canst tell how much he loveth thee. He has loved thee long; he has loved thee well, he loved thee ever; and he still shall love thee. Surely he is the person to comfort thee, because he loves. Admit him, then, to your heart, O Christian, that he may comfort you in your distress.

But next he is a *faithful* Comforter. Love sometimes

proveth unfaithful. "Oh! sharper than a serpent's tooth" is an unfaithful friend! Oh! far more bitter than the gall of bitterness, to have a friend to turn from me in my distress! Oh! woe of woes, to have one who loves me in my prosperity forsake me in the dark day of my trouble. Sad indeed: but such is not God's Spirit. He ever loves, and loves even to the end—a faithful Comforter. Child of God, you are in trouble. A little while ago you found him a sweet and loving Comforter; you obtained relief from him when others were but broken cisterns; he sheltered you in his bosom, and carried you in his arms. Oh, wherefore dost thou distrust him now? Away with thy fears! for he is a faithful Comforter. "Ah! but" thou sayest, "I fear I shall be sick and shall be deprived of his ordinances." Nevertheless, he shall visit thee on thy sick bed, and sit by thy side to give the consolation. "Ah! but I have distresses greater than you can conceive of; wave upon wave rolleth over me; deep calleth unto deep at the noise of the Eternal's waterspouts." Nevertheless, he will be faithful to his promise. "Ah! but I have sinned." So thou hast, but sin cannot sever thee from his love; he loves thee still. Think not, O poor downcast child of God, because the scars of thine old sins have marred thy beauty, that he loves thee less because of that blemish. Oh, no! He loved thee when he foreknew thy sin; he loved thee with the knowledge of what the aggregate of thy wickedness would be; and he does not love the less now. Come to him in all boldness of faith; tell him thou hast grieved him, and he will forget thy wandering, and will receive thee again; the kisses of his love shall be bestowed upon thee, and the arms of his grace shall embrace thee. He is faithful: trust him; he will never deceive you; trust him, he will never leave you.

Again, he is an *unwearied* Comforter. I have sometimes tried to comfort persons that have been tried. You now and then meet with the case of a nervous person. You ask, "What is your trouble?" You are told, and you essay, if possible, to remove it, but while you are preparing your artillery to batter the trouble, you find that it has shifted its quarters, and is occupying quite a different position. You change your argument and begin again; but lo, it is again gone, and you are bewildered. You feel like Hercules cutting off the ever-growing heads of the Hydra, and you give up your task in despair. You meet with persons whom it is impossible to comfort, reminding one of the man who locked himself up in fetters and threw the key away, so that nobody could unlock him. I have found some in the fetters of despair. "O, I am the man," say they, "that has seen affliction; pity me, pity me, O my friends;" and the more you try to comfort such people, the worse they get; and therefore, out of all heart, we leave them to wander alone among the tombs of their former joys. But the Holy Ghost is never out of heart with those whom he wishes to comfort. He attempts to comfort us and we run away from the sweet cordial; he gives some sweet draught to cure us, and we will not drink it; he gives some wondrous potion to charm away all our troubles, and we put it away from us. Still he pursues us; and though we say that we will not be comforted, he says we *shall* be, and when he has said, he does it; he is not to be wearied by all our sins, not by all our murmurings.

And oh, how *wise* a Comforter is the Holy Ghost. Job had comforters, and I think he spoke the truth when he said, "Miserable comforters are ye all." But I dare say they esteemed themselves wise; and when the young man Elihu rose to speak, they thought he had a world of impudence. Were they not "grave and reverend seniors?" Did not they comprehend his grief and sorrow? If they could not comfort him, who could? But they did not find out the cause. They thought he was not really a child of God, that he was self-righteous; and they gave him the wrong physic. It is a bad case when the doctor mistakes the disease and gives a wrong prescription, and so, perhaps, kills the patient. Sometimes, when we go and visit people we mistake their disease, we want to comfort them on this point, whereas they do not require any such comfort at all, and they would be better left alone than spoiled by such unwise comforters as we are. But oh! how wise the Holy Spirit is! he takes the soul, lays it on the table, and dissects it in a moment; he finds out the root of the matter, he sees where the complaint is, and then he applies the knife where something is required to be taken away, or puts a plaster where the sore it; and he never mistakes. Oh! how wise, the blessed Holy Ghost! from every comforter I turn and leave them all, for thou art he who alone givest the wisest consolation.

Then mark how *safe* a Comforter the Holy Ghost is. All comfort is not safe; mark that. There is a young man over there very melancholy. You know how he became so. He stepped into the house of God and heard a powerful preacher, and the word was blessed and convinced him of sin. When he went home, his father and the rest found there was something different about him, "Oh," they said, "John is mad; he is crazy;" and what said his mother? "Send him into the country for a week; let him go to the ball or to the theatre." John! Did you find any comfort there? "Ah, no; they made me worse, for while I was there, I thought hell might open and swallow me up." Did you find any relief in the gaities of the world? "No," say you, "I though, it was idle waste of time." Alas! this is miserable comfort, but it is the comfort of the worldling; and when a Christian gets into distress, how many will recommend him this remedy and the other. "Go and hear Mr. So-and-so preach; have a few friends at your house; read such-and-such a consoling volume; "and very likely it is the most unsafe advice in the world. The devil will sometimes come to men's souls as a false comforter, and he will say to the soul, "What need is there to make all this ado about repentance? you are no worse than other people," and he will try to make the soul believe that what is presumption is the real assurance of the Holy Ghost; thus he deceives many by false comfort. Ah, there have been many, like infants, destroyed by elixirs given to lull them to sleep; many have been ruined by the cry of "peace, peace," when there is no peace, hearing gentle things when they ought to be stirred to the quick. Cleopatra's asp was brought in a basket of flowers; and men's ruin often lurks in fair and sweet speeches. But the Holy Ghost's comfort is safe, and you may rest on it. Let him speak the word, and there is a reality about it; let him give the cup of consolation, and you may drink it to the bottom, for in its depths there are no dregs, nothing to intoxicate or ruin, it is all safe.

Moreover, the Holy Ghost is an *active* Comforter: he does not comfort by words, but by deeds. Some comfort by "Be ye warmed and be ye filled, giving nothing." But the Holy Ghost gives, he intercedes with Jesus; he gives us promises, he gives us grace, and so he comforts us. Mark again, he is always a *successful* Comforter; he never attempts what he cannot accomplish.

Then to close up, he is an *ever-present* Comforter, so that you never have to send for him. Your God is always near you, and when you need comfort in your distress, behold, the word is nigh thee, it is in thy mouth, and in thy heart; he is an ever-present help in time of trouble. I wish I had time to expand these thoughts; but I cannot.

II. The second thing is the COMFORT. Now there are some persons who make a great mistake about the influence of the Holy Spirit. A foolish man, who had a fancy to preach in a certain pulpit, though in truth he was quite incapable of the duty, called upon the minister, and assured him solemnly that it had been revealed to him by the Holy Ghost, that he was to preach in his pulpit. "Very well," said the minister, "I suppose I must not doubt your assertion, but as it has not been revealed to me that I am to let you preach, you must go your way until it is." I have heard many fanatical persons say the Holy Spirit revealed this and that to them. Now that is very generally revealed nonsense. The Holy Ghost does not reveal anything fresh now. He brings old things to our remembrance. "He shall teach you all things, and bring all things to your remembrance whatsoever I have told you." The canon of revelation is closed; there is no more to be added. God does not give a fresh revelation, but he rivets the old one. When it has been forgotten, and laid in the dusty chamber of our memory, he fetches it out and cleans the picture, but does not paint a new one. There are no new doctrines, but the old ones are often revived. It is not, I say, by any new revelation that the Spirit comforts. He does so by telling us old things over again; he brings a fresh lamp to manifest the treasures hidden in Scripture; he unlocks the strong chests in which the truth had long lain, and he points to secret chambers filled with untold riches; but he coins no more, for enough is done. Believer! there is enough in the Bible for thee to live upon for ever. If thou shouldst outnumber the years of Methusaleh, there would be no need for a fresh revelation; if thou shouldst live till Christ should come upon the earth, there would be no necessity for the addition of a single word; if thou shouldst go down as deep as Jonah, or even descend as David said he did, into the belly of hell, still there would be enough in the Bible to comfort thee without a supplementary sentence. But Christ says, "He shall take of mine and shall show it unto you." Now let me just tell you briefly what it is the Holy Ghost tells us.

Ah! does he not whisper to the heart, "Saint, be of good cheer; there is one who died for thee; look to Calvary; behold his wounds; see the torrent gushing from his side; there is thy purchaser, and thou art secure. He loves thee with an everlasting love, and this chastisement is meant for thy good; each stroke is working thy healing; by the blueness of the wound thy soul is made better. "Whom he loveth he chasteneth, and scourgeth every son whom he receiveth." Doubt not his grace, because of thy tribulation, but believe that he loveth thee as much in seasons of trouble as in times of happiness." And then, moreover, he says, "What is all thy suffering compared with that of thy

Lord's? or what, when weighed in the scales of Jesu's agonies, is all thy distress?" And especially at times does the Holy Ghost take back the veil of heaven, and lets the soul behold the glory of the upper world! then it is that the saint can say, "Oh, thou art a Comforter to me!"

"Let cares like a wild deluge come,
    And storms of sorrow fall;
May I but safely reach my home,
    My God, my heaven, my all."

Some of you could follow, were I to tell of manifestations of heaven. You too have left sun, moon, and stars, at your feet, while in your flight, outstripping the tardy lightning, you have seemed to enter the gates of pearl, and tread the golden streets, borne aloft on wings of the Spirit. But here we must not trust ourselves, lest, lost in reverie, we forget our theme.

III. And now thirdly, who are the COMFORTED persons! I like, you know at the end of my sermon to cry out "Divide! divide!" There are two parties here—some who are the comforted, and others who are the comfortless ones—some who have have received the consolation of the Holy Ghost, and some who have not. Now let us try and sift you, and see which is the chaff, and which is the wheat; and may God grant that some of the chaff may this night be transformed into his wheat.

You may say, "How am I to know whether I am a recipient of the comfort of the Holy Ghost?" You may know it by one rule. If you have received one blessing from God, you will receive all other blessings too. Let me explain myself. If I could come here as an auctioneer, and sell the gospel off in lots, I should dispose of it all. If I could say here is justification through the blood of Christ, free, giving away, gratis; many a one would say, "I will have justification: give it me; I wish to be justified, I wish to be pardoned." Suppose I took sanctification, the giving up of all sin, a thorough change of heart, leaving off drunkenness and swearing, many would say, "I don't want that; I should like to go to heaven, but I do not want that holiness; I should like to be saved at last, but I should like to have my drink still; I should like to enter glory, but then I must have an oath or two on the road." Nay, but sinner, if thou hast one blessing, thou shalt have all. God will never divide the gospel. He will not give justification to that man, and sanctification to another; pardon to one and holiness to another. No, it all goes together. Whom he calls them he justifies; whom he justifies, them he sanctifies; and whom he sanctifies, them he also glorifies. Oh; if I could lay down nothing but the *comforts* of the gospel, ye would fly to them as flies do to honey. When ye come to be ill, ye send for the clergyman. Ah! you all want your minister then to come and give you consoling words. But if he be an honest man, he will not give some of you a particle of consolation. He will not commence pouring oil when the knife would be better. I want to make a man feel his sins before I dare tell him anything about Christ. I want to probe into his soul and make him feel that he is lost before I tell him anything about the purchased blessing. It is the ruin of many to tell them. "Now just believe on Christ, and that is all you have to do." If, instead of dying they get better, they rise up whitewashed hypocrites—that is all. I have heard of a city missionary who kept a record of two thousand persons who were supposed to be on their death-bed, but recovered, and whom he should have put down as converted persons had they died, and how many do you think lived a Christian life afterwards out of the two-thousand! Not two! Positively he could only find one who was found to live afterwards in the fear of God. Is it not horrible that when men and women come to die, they should cry, "Comfort, comfort?" and that hence their friends conclude that they are children of God, while after all they have no right to consolation, but are intruders upon the enclosed grounds of the blessed God. O God! may these people ever be kept from having comfort when they have no right to it! Have you the other blessings? Have you had conviction of sin? Have you ever felt your guilt before God? Have your souls been humbled at Jesus' feet? And have you been made to look to Calvary alone for your refuge? If not, you have no right to consolation. Do not take an atom of it. The Spirit is a Convincer before he is a Comforter; and you must have the other operations of the Holy Spirit, before you can derive anything from this.

And now I have done. You have heard what this babbler hath said once more. What has it been? Something about the Comforter. But let me ask you, before you go, what do you know about the Comforter? Each one of you before descending the steps of this chapel, let this solemn question thrill through your souls—What do you know of the Comforter? Oh! poor souls, if ye know not the Comforter, I will tell you what you shall know—You shall know the Judge! If ye know not the Comforter on earth, ye shall know the Condemner in the next world, who shall cry, "Depart ye cursed into everlasting fire in hell." Well might Whitfield call out, "O earth, earth, earth, hear the Word of the Lord!" If we were to live here for ever, ye might slight the gospel; if ye had a lease of your lives, ye might despise the Comforter. But sirs, ye must die. Since last we met together, probably some have gone to their long last home; and ere we meet again in this sanctuary, some here will be amongst the glorified above, or amongst the damned below. Which will it be? Let your soul answer. If to-night you fell down dead in your pews, or where you are standing in the gallery, where would you be? in *heaven* or in *hell*? Ah! deceive not yourselves; let conscience have its perfect work; and if, in the sight of God, you are obliged to say, "I tremble and fear lest my portion should be with unbelievers," listen one moment, and then I have done with thee. "He that believeth and is baptized shall be saved, and he that believeth not shall be damned." Weary sinner, hellish sinner, thou who art the devil's castaway, reprobate, profligate, harlot, robber, thief, adulterer, fornicator, drunkard, swearer, Sabbath-breaker—list! I speak to thee as well as the rest. I exempt no man. God hath said there is no exemption here. "*Whosoever* believeth in the name of Jesus Christ shall be saved." Sin is no barrier: thy guilt is no obstacle. Whosoever—though he were as black as Satan, though he were filthy as a fiend—whosoever this night believes, shall have every sin forgiven, shall have every crime effaced, shall have every iniquity blotted out; shall be saved in the Lord Jesus Christ, and shall stand in heaven safe and secure. That is the glorious gospel. God apply it home to your hearts, and give you faith in Jesus!

"We have listened to the preacher—
    Truth by him has now been shown;
But we want a GREATER TEACHER,
    From the everlasting throne:
        APPLICATION
    Is the work of God *alone*."

6
THE SUPERLATIVE EXCELLENCE OF THE HOLY SPIRIT

"Nevertheless I tell you the truth; it is expedient for you that I go away: for if I go not away, the Comforter will not come unto you; but if I depart, I will send him unto you."—John 16:7.

~

THE saints of God may very justly reckon their losses among their greatest gains. The adversities of believers minister much to their prosperity. Although we know this, yet through the infirmity of the flesh we tremble at soul-enriching afflictions, and dread to see those black ships which bring us such freights of golden treasure. When the Holy Spirit sanctifies the furnace, the flame refines our gold and consumes our dross, yet the dull ore of our nature likes not the glowing coals, and had rather lie quiet in the dark mines of earth. As silly children cry because they are called to drink the medicine which will heal their sicknesses, even so do we. Our gracious Saviour, however, loves us too wisely to spare us the trouble because of our childish fears; he foresees the advantage which will spring from our griefs, and therefore thrusts us into them out of wisdom and true affection. It was a very great trouble to these first apostles to lose their teacher and friend. Sorrow had filled their heart at the thought that he should depart, but yet his departure was to give them the greater blessing of the Holy Spirit; and therefore their entreaties and tears cannot avert the dreaded separation. Christ will not gratify their wishes at so vast an expense as the withholding of the Spirit. Mourn as they may under the severe trial, Jesus will not remain with them, because his departure is in the highest degree expedient. Beloved, let us expect to be subject to the same loving discipline. Let us reckon upon losing happy frames and choice enjoyments when Jesus knows that the loss will be better for us than the enjoyment.

God has given two great gifts to his people: the first is, *his Son for us;* the second is, *his Spirit to us.* After he had given his Son for us, to become incarnate, to work righteousness, and to offer an atonement, that gift had been fully bestowed, and there remained no more to be conferred in that respect. "It is finished!" proclaimed the completion of atonement, and his resurrection showed the perfection of justification. It was not therefore necessary that Christ should remain any longer upon earth since his work below is for ever finished. Now is the season for the second gift, the descent of the Holy Spirit. This could not be bestowed until Christ had ascended, because this choice favour was reserved to grace with highest honour the triumphant ascension of the great Redeemer. "When he ascended up on high, he led captivity captive, and gave gifts unto men." This was, as Peter tells us, the great promise which Jesus received of his Father. "Therefore being by the right hand of God exalted, and having received of the Father the promise of the Holy Ghost, he hath shed forth this, which ye now see and hear." That his triumphal entrance into heaven might be stamped with signal glory, the gifts of the Spirit of God could not be scattered among the sons of men until the Lord had gone up with a shout, even the Lord with the sound of trumpet.

The first gift being completed, it became necessary that he whose person and work make up that priceless boon should withdraw himself that he might have power to distribute the second benefit by which alone the first gift becomes of any service to us. Christ crucified is of no practical value to us without the work of the Holy Spirit; and the atonement which Jesus wrought can never save a single soul unless the blessed Spirit of God shall apply it to the heart and conscience. Jesus is never seen until the Holy Spirit opens the eye: the water from the well of life is never received until the Holy Spirit has drawn it from the depths. As medicine unused for want of the physician's word; as sweets untasted because out of reach; as treasure unvalued because hidden in the earth; such is Jesus the Saviour, until the Holy Spirit teaches us to know him, and applies his blood to our souls.

It is to the honour of the Holy Spirit that I desire to speak this morning, and O may the same hallowed flame which of old sat upon the apostles, now rest upon the preacher, and may the Word come with power to our hearts.

I. We shall commence our discourse by the remark, that THE BODILY PRESENCE OF CHRIST MUST HAVE BEEN EXCEEDINGLY PRECIOUS. *How* precious those alone can tell who love Christ much. Love always desires to be in the company of the thing beloved, and absence causes grief. What is fully meant by the expression, "Sorrow hath filled your heart," those only can know who anticipate a like painful bereavement. Jesus had become the joy of their eyes, the sun of their days, the star of their nights: like the spouse, as she came up from the wilderness, they leaned upon their beloved. They were as little children, and now that their Lord and Master was going they felt they should be left orphans. Well might they have great sorrow of heart. So much love, so much sorrow, when the object of love is withdrawn. Judge ye, my brethren, the joy which the bodily presence of Christ would give to us this morning, and then you can tell how precious it must be. Have we not, some of us, been looking for years for the personal advent of Christ? We have lifted up our eyes in the morning and we have said, "Perhaps he will come this day," and when the day has closed we have continued our watching in our sleepless hours, and renewed our hopes with the rising of the sun. We longingly expect him according to his promise; and like men who watch for their Lord, we stand with loins girt about waiting for his appearing. We are looking for and hastening unto the day of the Lord. This is the bright hope which cheers the Christian, the hope that the Saviour shall descend to reign amongst his people gloriously. Suppose him to appear suddenly on this platform now, how would you clap your hands. Why, the lame among you would, at the joy of his appearance, leap like a hart, and even the dumb might sing for joy. The presence of the Master! What rapture! Come quickly! Come quickly, Lord Jesus! It must be indeed a precious thing to enjoy the corporeal presence of Christ.

Think of the advantage it would be in the instruction of his people. No mystery need puzzle us if we could refer all to him. The disputes of the Christian Church would soon be ended for he would tell us what his Word meant beyond dispute. There would be no discouragement to the Church henceforth in her work of faith and labour of love, for the presence of Christ would be the end of all difficulties, and insure conquest over all enemies. We should not have to mourn as we now do over our forgetfulness of Jesus, for we should sometimes catch a look at him; and a sight of him would give us a store of joy, so that like the prophet of Horeb, we could go forty days in the strength of that meat. It were a delightful thing to know that Christ was somewhere upon earth, for then he would take the personal supervision of his universal Church. He could warn us of apostates; he could reject the hypocrites; he would comfort the feeble-minded, and rebuke the erring. How delightful would it be to see him walking among the golden candlesticks, holding the stars in his right hand. Churches need not then be subdivided and rent with evil passions. Christ would create unity. Schism would cease to be, and heresy would be rooted out. The presence of Jesus, whose countenance is as the sun shining in his strength, would ripen all the fruits of our garden, consume all the weeds, and quicken every plant. The two-edged sword of his mouth would slay his foes, and his eyes of fire would kindle the holy passions of his friends.

But I shall not enlarge upon that point, because it is one in which fancy exercises itself at the expense of judgment. I question whether the pleasure which the thought of Christ's being here in the flesh has given us just now, may not have had a leaven of carnality in it. I question whether the Church is yet prepared to enjoy the corporeal presence of her Saviour, without falling into the error of knowing him after the flesh. It may be it shall need centuries of education before the Church is fit to see her Saviour in the flesh on earth again, because I see in my own self—and I suppose it is so in you—that much of the delight which I expect from the company of Christ, is according to the sight of the eyes and the judgment of the mind; and sight is ever the mark and symbol of the flesh.

II. However, leaving that point, we come to the second, which is, THAT THE PRESENCE OF THE COMFORTER, AS WE HAVE IT UPON EARTH, IS VERY MUCH BETTER THAN THE BODILY PRESENCE OF CHRIST.

We have fancied that the bodily presence of Christ would make us blessed, and confer innumerable boons; but according to our text, the presence of the Holy Ghost working in the Church, is more expedient for the Church. I think this will be clear to you, if you think for a moment, that the bodily presence of Christ on the earth, however good it might be for the Church, would in our present condition involve many inconveniences which are avoided by his presence through the Holy Spirit. Christ, being most truly man, must as to his manhood inhabit a certain place, and in order to get to Christ, it would be necessary for us to travel to his place of residence. Conceive all men compelled to travel from the ends of the earth to visit the Lord Jesus Christ, dwelling upon Mount Zion, or in the city of Jerusalem. What a lengthened voyage would that be for those who live in the far-off ends of the world. Doubtless they would joyfully undertake it, and as peace would be universal, and poverty be banished, men might not be restrained from taking such a journey, but might all be able to accomplish it; yet as they could not all live where they could every morning see Christ, they must be content with every now and then getting a glimpse of him. But see, my brethren, the Holy Spirit, the vicar of Christ, dwells everywhere; and if we wish to apply to the Holy Spirit, we have no need to move an inch; in the closet we can find him, or in the streets we can talk with him. Jesus Christ could not be present in this congregation after the flesh, and yet present in a neighbouring Church, much less present in America, and in Australia, and in Europe, and in Africa, at the same time; but the Holy Spirit is everywhere, and through that Holy Spirit Christ keeps his promise, "Where two or three are met together in my name, there am I in the midst of them." He could not keep that promise according to the flesh, at least, we are quite unable to conceive of his so doing; but through the Holy Spirit we sweetly enjoy his presence, and hope to do so to the world's end.

Think again, access to Christ if he were here in his corporeal personality, would not be very easy to all believers. There are only twenty-four hours in the day, and if our Lord never slept, if, as a man, he could still live, and, like the saints above, rest not day nor night, yet there are only the twenty-four hours; and what were twenty-four hours for the supervision of a Church which we trust will cover the whole earth? How could a thousand millions of believers all receive immediate personal comfort either from his lips or the smiles of his face? Even at the present moment, there are some millions of true saints upon earth—what could one man do by his personal presence, even though that one man were incarnate Deity? what could he do in one day for the comfort of all of these? Why, we could not possibly expect each one of us to see him every day—nay, we could scarcely expect to have our turn once in the year. But, beloved, we can now see Jesus every hour and every moment of every hour. So often as ye bow the knee, his Spirit, who represents him, can commune with you and bless you. No matter whether it be at the dead of night that your cry goes up, or under the blaze of burning noon, there is the Spirit waiting to be gracious, and your sighs and cries climb up to Christ in heaven, and return with answers of peace. These difficulties did not occur to you, perhaps, in your first thinkings; but if you meditate awhile, you will see that the presence of the Spirit, avoiding that difficulty, makes Christ accessible to every saint at all times; not to a few choice favourites, but to every believing man and woman the Holy Ghost is accessible, and thus the whole body of the faithful can enjoy present and perpetual communion with Christ.

We ought to consider yet once more, that Christ's presence in the flesh upon the earth, for any other purpose than that of ending the present dispensation, would involve another difficulty. Of course every word which Christ had spoken from the time of the apostles until now would have been inspired; being inspired it would have been a thousand pities that it should fall to the ground. Busy scribes would therefore be always taking down Christ's words; and, my brethren, if in the short course of three years our Saviour managed to do and to say so much that one of the Evangelists informs us, that if all had been written the world itself could not have contained the books which would have been written, I ask you to imagine what a mass of literature the Christian Church would have acquired if she had preserved the words of Christ throughout these one thousand eight hundred and sixty-four years? Certainly we should not have had the Word of God in the simple compact form of a pocket Bible, it would have consisted of innumerable volumes of the sayings and deeds of the Lord Jesus Christ. Only the studious, nay, not even the studious could have read all the Lord's teachings, and the poor and the illiterate must ever have been at a great disadvantage. But now we have a book which is finished within a narrow compass with not another line to be added to it; the canon of revelation is sealed up for ever, and the poorest man in England believing in Christ, going with a humble soul to that book, and looking up to Jesus Christ who is present through his Spirit though not after the flesh, may, in a short time, comprehend the doctrines of grace, and understand with all saints what are the heights and depths, and know the love of Christ which passeth knowledge. So then, on the score of inconvenience, precious as the corporeal presence of Christ might be, it is infinitely better for the Church's good that, until the day of her millennial glory, Christ should be present by his Spirit, and not in the flesh.

Yet more, my brethren, if Jesus Christ were still present with his Church in the flesh, *the life of faith* would not have such room for its display as it now has. The more there is visible to the eye, the less room for faith: the least faith the most show. The Romish Church, which has little enough of true faith, provides everything to work upon the senses; your nostrils are regaled with incense, and your ears are delighted with sweet sounds. The more faith grows, the less it needs outward helps; and when faith shows her true character, and is clean divorced from sense and sight, then she wants absolutely nothing to rest upon but the invisible power of God; she has learned to hang as the world hangeth, upon no seen support; just as the eternal arch of you blue sky springs right up without props, so faith rests upon the invisible pillars of God's truth and faithfulness, needing nothing to shore or buttress her. The presence of Christ Jesus here in bodily flesh, and the knowing of him according to the flesh, would be the bringing back of the saints to a life of sight, and in a measure spoil the simplicity of naked trust. You remember the apostle Paul says, "We now know no man after the flesh; yea," says he, "though we have known Christ after the flesh, yet now after the flesh know we him no more." To the sceptic, who should ask us, "Why do you believe in Christ?" if Jesus had remained upon the earth, we could always give an easy answer—"There he is—there is the man. Behold him as he continues still to work miracles." There would be very little room for faith's holy adherence to the bare Word of God, and no opportunity for her to glorify God, trusting where she cannot trace: but now, beloved, the fact that we have nothing visible to point to which carnal minds can understand—this very fact makes the path of faith more truly congenial with its noble character.

"Faith, mighty faith, the promise sees,
And looks to that alone;"

which she could hardly do, if she could look upon the visible person of a present Saviour. Happy day will it be for us when faith enjoys the full fruition of her hopes in the triumphant advent of her Lord; but his absence alone can train and educate her to the needed point of spiritual refinement.

Furthermore, the presence of Jesus Christ on earth would materially affect the character of God's great battle against error and sin. Suppose that Christ were to destroy the preachers of error by miracle; suppose that persecuting monarchs had their arms dried up, or that all men who would oppose Christ were suddenly devoured by fire, why then it would be rather a battle between physical greatness and moral evil, than a warfare in which only spiritual force is employed on the side of right. But now that Christ has gone, the fight is all between spirit and spirit; between God the Holy Spirit and Satan; between truth and error; between the earnestness of believing men and the infatuation of unbelieving men. Now the fight is fair. We have no miracle on our side—we do not want it, the Holy Spirit is enough; we call no fire from heaven—no earthquake shakes the ground beneath our foemen's feet; Korah is not swallowed up; Dathan does not go down alive into the pit. Physical force is left to our enemies, we ask it not. Why? Because by the divine working we can vanquish error without it. In the name of the Holy One of Israel, in whose cause we have been enlisted—by *his* might we are enough without miracles, and signs, and wonders. If Christ were here still working miracles, the battle were not so spiritual as it now is; but the absence of the corporeal Saviour makes it a spiritual conflict of spirit of the noblest and sublimest order.

Again, dear friends, the Holy Spirit is more valuable to the Church in her present militant state than the presence of Christ could be conceived to be, because Christ must be here in one of two ways—either he must be here suffering, or not suffering. If Christ were here suffering, then how could we conclude that his atonement was finished? Is it not much better for our faith that our blessed Lord, having once for all made expiation for sin, should sit at the right hand of the Father? Is it not much better, I ask, than to see him still struggling and suffering here below? "Oh! but," you say, "perhaps he would not suffer!" Then I pray you, do not wish to have him here till our warfare is accomplished, for to see an unsuffering Christ in the midst of his suffering people—to see his face calm and clear when yours and mine are wrinkled with grief—to see him smiling when we are weeping, this were intolerable; no, it could not be. Brethren, if he be a suffering Christ in our sight, then we should suspect that he had not finished his work; and, on the other hand, if he be an unsuffering Christ, then it would look as if he were not a faithful High Priest made like unto his brethren. These two difficulties throw us back into a state of thankfulness to God that we have not the dilemma to answer, but that the Spirit of God, who is Christ present on earth, relieves us from these difficulties and gives us all the advantage we could expect from Christ's presence in a tenfold degree.

Only this one further remark, that the personal presence of Christ, much as we think of it, did not produce very great results in his disciples until the Spirit was poured forth from on high. Christ was their Teacher—how much did they learn? Why, there is Philip—Christ has to say to him, "Have I been so long time with you, and yet hast thou not known me, Philip?" They were puzzled by questions which little children can now answer; you can see that at the end of their three years' course of training with Christ, they had made but slender progress. Christ is not only their Teacher, but their Comforter; yet how frequently Christ failed to console them, because of their unbelief. After he had uttered that delightful discourse which we have been reading, he found them sleeping for sorrow. In this very chapter, when he is trying to comfort them, he adds, "But because I have said these things unto you, sorrow hath filled your heart." Christ's object was to foster the graces of his disciples—but where were their graces? Here is Peter—he has not even the grace of courage and consistency, but denies his Master while the rest of them forsake him and fly. There was not even the Spirit of Christ infused into them. Their zeal was not tempered with love, for they wanted fire from heaven to consume his adversaries, and Peter drew a sword to cut off the high-priest's servant's ear. They scarcely knew the truths which their Master taught, and they were far enough from imbibing his heavenly Spirit. Even their endowments were slender. It is true they once wrought miracles, and preached, but with what success? Do you ever hear of Peter winning three thousand sinners under a sermon till the Holy Spirit came? Do you find any of them able to edify others, and build up the Church of Christ? No, the ministry of our Lord Jesus Christ, considered only as to its immediate fruits, was not to be compared with ministries after the descent of the Spirit. "He came unto his own, and his own received him not." His great work as a Redeemer was a complete triumph from beginning to end; but as a Teacher, since the Spirit of God was only upon *him*, and not upon the people, his words were rejected, his entreaties were despised, and his warnings unheeded by the great multitude of the people. The mighty blessing came when the words of Joel were fulfilled. "And it shall come to pass afterward, that I will pour out my Spirit upon all flesh; and your sons and your daughters shall prophesy, your old men shall dream dreams, your young men shall see visions: and also upon the servants and upon the handmaids in those days will I pour out my Spirit." That was the blessing, and a blessing which, we venture to say again, was so rich and so rare that it was indeed expedient that Jesus Christ should go that the Holy Spirit might descend.

III. I now pass on to the third point of the subject with brevity. We have come thus far—the presence of Christ admitted to be precious, but the presence of the Holy Spirit most clearly shown to be of more practical value to the Church of God than the corporeal presence of the Lord Jesus Christ. Advance then to the third point, THE PRESENCE OF THE COMFORTER IS SUPERLATIVELY VALUABLE. We may gather this first from the effects which were seen upon the day of Pentecost. On the day of Pentecost the heavenly tocsin sounded the alarm of war. The soldiers were ill prepared for it; they were a slender band, having only this virtue, that they were content to wait until power was given to them. They sat still in the upper room. That mighty sound was heard across Jerusalem. The forceful whirlwind travels on until it reaches the chosen spot. It fills the place where they are sitting. Here was an omen of what the Spirit of God is to be to the Church. It is to come mysteriously upon the

Church according to the sovereign will of God; but when he comes like the wind, it is to purge the moral atmosphere, and to quicken the pulse of all who spiritually breathe. This is a blessing indeed, a boon which the Church greatly wants; I would that this rushing mighty wind would come upon this Church with an irresistible force, which should carry everything before it—the force of truth, but of more than truth, the force of God driving truth home upon the heart and conscience of men. I would that you and I could breathe this wind, and receive its invigorating influence, that we might be made champions of God and of his truth. O that it would drive away our mists of doubt and clouds of error. Come, sacred wind, England needs thee—the whole earth requires thee. The foul miasmas which brood in this deadly calm would fly if thy divine lightnings enlightened the world, and set the moral atmosphere in commotion. Come, Holy Spirit, come, we can do nothing without thee; but if we have thy wind, we spread our sail, and speed onward towards glory.

Then the Spirit came as fire. A fire-shower accompanied the rushing mighty wind. What a blessing is this to the Church! The Church wants fire to quicken her ministers, to give zeal and energy to all her members. Having this fire, she burns her way to success. The world meets her with the fire of faggots, but she confronts the world with the fire of kindling spirits and of souls aglow with the love of Jesus Christ. She trusts not to the wit, and eloquence, and wisdom of her preachers, but to the divine fire which clothes them with energy. She knows that men are irresistible when they are filled with hallowed enthusiasm sent from God. She trusts therefore in this, and her cry is, "Come, holy fire, abide upon our pastors and teachers! rest upon every one of us!" This fire is a blessing Christ did not bring us in person, but which he now gives through his Spirit to the Church.

Then there came from the fire-shower a descent of tongues. This, too, is the privilege of the Church. When the Lord gave the apostles divers tongues, he did, as it were, give them the keys of the various kingdoms. "Go," saith he, "Judea is not my only dominion, go and unlock the gates of every empire, here are the keys, you can speak every language." Dear friends, though we can no longer speak with every man in his own tongue, yet we have the keys of the whole world swinging at our girdle if we have the Spirit of God with us. You have the keys of human hearts if the Spirit of God speaks through you. <u>I have this day the keys of the hearts of the multitudes here if the Holy Spirit wills to use them!</u> There is an efficacy about the gospel, when the Spirit is with us, little dreamed of by those who call it the foolishness of men. I am persuaded that the results which have followed ministry in our lifetime are trivial and insignificant, compared with what they would be if the Spirit of God were more mightily at work in our midst. There is no reason in the nature of the gospel or the power of the Spirit, why a whole congregation should not be converted under one sermon. There is no reason in God's nature why a nation should not be born in a day, and why, within a single twelve months, a dozen ministers preaching throughout the world, might not be the means of converting every elect son and daughter of Adam to a knowledge of the truth. The Spirit of God is perfectly irresistible when he puts forth his full power. His power is so divinely omnipotent that the moment he goeth forth the work is achieved. The great prophetic event, we see, occcurred on the day of Pentecost. The success given was only the first fruits— Pentecost is not the harvest. We have been accustomed to look on Pentecost as a great and wonderful display of divine power, not at all to be equalled in modern times. Brethren, it is to be exceeded. I stand not upon Pentecost as upon a towering mountain, wondering at my height, but I look at Pentecost as a little rising knoll from which I am to look up to mountains loftier far. I look not to Pentecost as the shouting of our harvest-home, and the bringing in of the sheaves into the garner, no, but as an offering of the first wave sheaf before the altar of God. You must expect greater things, pray for greater things, long for greater things. Here is this England of ours, sunk in stolid ignorance of the gospel. Weighing like a nightmare upon her bosom we have baptismal regeneration, supported by a horde of priests, who either believe that dogma, or hold their benefices by subscribing to a lie. How is this incubus to be shaken off from the living bosom of England? "Not by might, nor by power, but by my Spirit, saith the Lord." There is France cursed with infidelity, fickle, gay, given up to pleasure—how is she to be made sober and sanctified unto God?—"Not by might, but by my Spirit, saith the Lord." Yonder is Germany, with her metaphysical scepticism, her half-Romanism, that is to say, Lutheranism, and her abounding Popery; how is she to arise? "Not by might, nor by power, but by my Spirit, saith the Lord." Away there in Italy sits old Rome, the harlot of the seven hills, still reigning queen triumphant over the great part of the earth; how is she to die? Where is the sword which shall find out her heart? "Not by might, nor by power, but by my Spirit, saith the Lord." The one thing then which we want, is the Spirit of God. Do not say that we want money; we shall have it soon enough when the Spirit touches men's hearts. Do not say that we want buildings, churches, edifices; all these may be very well in subserviency, but the main want of the Church is the Spirit, and men into whom the Spirit may be poured. If there were only one prayer which I might pray before I died, it should be this; "Lord, send thy Church men filled with the Holy Ghost, and with fire." Give to any denomination such men, and its progress must be mighty: keep back such men, send them college gentlemen, of great refinement and profound learning, but of little fire and grace, dumb dogs which cannot bark, and straightway that denomination must decline. Let the Spirit come, and the preacher may be rustic, simple, rough, unmannered, but the Holy Ghost being upon him, none of his adversaries shall stand against him; his word shall be with power to the shaking of the gates of hell. Beloved, did I not say well, when I said that the Spirit of God is of superlative importance to the Church, and that the day of Pentecost seems to tell us this?

Remember, brethren, and here is another thought which should make the Spirit very dear to you, that without the Holy Spirit no good thing ever did or ever can come into any of your hearts—no sigh of penitence—no cry of faith—no glance of love—no tear of hallowed sorrow. Your heart can never palpitate with life divine, except through the Spirit; you are not capable of the smallest degree of spiritual emotion, much less spiritual action, apart from the Holy Ghost. Dead you lie, living only for evil, but absolutely dead for God until the Holy Ghost comes and raises you from the grave. There is nothing good in you today, my brother, which was not put there. The flowers of Christ are all exotics—"In me, that is, in my flesh, dwelleth no good thing." "Who can bring a clean thing out of an unclean? not one." Everything must come from Christ, and Christ gives nothing to men except through the Spirit of all grace. Prize, then, the Spirit as the channel of all good which cometh into you.

And further, no good thing can come out of you apart from the Spirit. Let it be in you, yet it lies dormant except God worketh in you to will and to do of his own good pleasure. Do you desire to preach?—how can you unless the Holy Ghost touches your tongue? Do you desire to pray? Alas! what dull work it is unless the Spirit maketh intercession for you. Do you desire to subdue sin? Would you be holy? Would you imitate your Master? Do you desire to rise to superlative heights of spirituality? Are you wanting to be made like the angels of God, full of zeal and ardour for the Master's cause? You cannot without the Spirit—"Without me ye can do nothing." O branch of the vine, thou canst have no fruit without the sap! O child of God, thou hast no life within thee apart from the life which God gives thee through his Spirit! Said I not well, then, that the Holy Spirit is superlatively precious, so that even the presence of Christ after the flesh is not to be compared to his presence for glory and for power?

IV. This brings us to the conclusion, which is a practical point. Brethren, if these things be so, let us, who are believers in Christ, view the mysterious Spirit with deep awe and reverence. Let us so reverence him as not to grieve him or provoke him to anger by our sin. Let us not quench him in one of his faintest motions in our soul; let us foster every suggestion, and be ready to obey every prompting. If the Holy Spirit be indeed so mighty, let us do nothing without him; let us begin no project, and carry on no enterprise, and conclude no transaction, without imploring his blessing. Let us do him the due homage of feeling our entire weakness apart from him, and then depending alone upon him, having this for our prayer, "Open thou my heart, and my whole being to thine incoming, and uphold me with thy free spirit when I shall have received that spirit in my inward parts."

You who are unconverted, let me beseech you, whatever you do, never despise the Spirit of God. Remember, there is a special honour put upon him in Scripture—"All manner of sin and of blasphemy shall be forgiven unto men, but the sin against the Holy Ghost shall never be forgiven, neither in this world nor in that which is to come." Remember, "If a man speak a word against the Son of Man, it shall be forgiven him; but if he speak a word against the Holy Ghost, it shall never be forgiven him." This is the sin which is unto death, of which even the loving John says: "I do not say that ye shall pray for it." Tremble, therefore, in his presence, put off your shoes from off your feet, for when his name is mentioned, the place whereon thou standest is holy ground. Let the Spirit be treated with reverence.

In the next place, as a practical remark, let us, viewing the might of the Spirit, take courage to-day. We know, brethren, that we as a body of people, seeking to adhere closely to Scripture and to practise the ordinances and hold the doctrines as we have received them from the Lord himself, are but poor and despised; and when we look at the great ones of the earth, we see them on the side of the false and not of the true. Where are the kings and the nobles? Where are the princes, and where are the mighty men? Are they not against the Lord of Hosts. Where is the gold? where is the silver? where is the architecture? where is the wisdom? where is the eloquence? Is it not banded against the Lord of Hosts? What then! shall we be discouraged?—our fathers were not. They bore their testimony in the stocks and in the prison, but they feared not for the good old cause; as like John Bunyan, they learned to rot in dungeons, but they learned not to play the coward. They suffered, and they testified that they were not discouraged. Why? because they knew (not that truth is mighty and will prevail, for truth is not mighty and will not prevail in this world until men are different from what they are), but they knew that the Spirit of God is mighty and will prevail. Better to have a small Church of poor men and the Spirit of God with them, than to have a hierarchy of nobles, to have an army of titled princes and prelates without the Holy Spirit, for this is not merely the sinew of strength, but it is strength itself—where the Spirit of God is there is liberty and power. Courage then, brethren, we have only to seek for that which God has promised to give, and we can do wonders. He will give the Holy Spirit to them that ask him. Wake up, members of this Church, to earnest prayer; and all believers throughout the world, cry aloud unto God to let his bare arm be seen. Wake, children of God, for ye know the power of prayer. Give the covenant angel no rest till he speak the word, and the Spirit worketh mightily among the sons of men. Prayer is work adapted to each of you who are in Christ. You cannot preach, you cannot teach, but you can pray; and your private prayer, unknown by men, shall be registered in heaven; those silent but earnest cries of yours shall bring down a blessing. The other morning, when we were holding special prayer, there were some brethren present who kept saying during the prayer to themselves, scarcely loud enough to be heard, "Do Lord! Do! Grant it! Hear it!" That is a kind of praying which I love in prayer meetings; I would not care for the loud shouts of some of our Methodist brethren, though if they like they are welcome to it, but I do like to hear friends praying with the groaning which cannot be uttered, "Lord, send the Spirit! Send the Spirit, Lord! Work! Work! Work!" During sermon time it is what numbers of Churches should be doing, crying out to God in their hearts. As you walk the streets when you see sin you should pray, "Lord, put it down by thy Spirit!" and when you mark a struggling brother striving to do good, you should cry, "Lord, help him! help him by thy Spirit." I am persuaded we only want more prayer, and there is no limit to the blessing; you may evangelize England, you may evangelize Europe, you may Christianize the world, if ye do but know how to pray. Prayer can get anything of God, prayer can get everything: God denies nothing to the man who knows how to ask; the Lord never shuts his storehouse till you shut your mouth; God will never stop his arm till you stop your tongue. Cry aloud and spare not; give him no rest till he sendeth forth his Spirit once again to stir the waters, and to brood over this dark world till light and life shall come. Cry day and night, O ye elect of God, for he will avenge you speedily. The time of battle draweth nigh. Rome sharpens her sword for the fight, the men of error gnash their teeth in rage. Now for the sword of the Lord and of Gideon! Now for the old might, and majesty of the ancient days! Now for the shaking of the walls of Jericho, even though we have no better weapons than rams' horns! Now for the driving out of the heathen, and for the establishment of God's Israel in the land! Now for the coming of the Holy Spirit with such might and power, that as Noah's flood covered the mountain-tops, Jehovah's flood of glory shall cover the highest summits of sin and iniquity, and the whole world over the Lord God Omnipotent shall reign.

You who have not the Spirit pray for it. May he prompt you to pray this morning! Unconverted sinners, may the Spirit give you faith; remember that the Holy Spirit tells you to trust Christ. If you honour the Holy Spirit, trust Christ. I know you must be regenerate, but the man who trusts Christ is regenerate. You must repent, you must be holy, but the man who trusts Christ shall repent and shall be made holy; the germs of repentance and holiness are in him already. Trust Christ, sinner; it is the Holy Ghost's mandate to you this morning. May he constrain you to trust him, and he shall have the glory, world without end. Amen.

7
THE HOLY SPIRIT'S THREEFOLD CONVICTION OF MEN

"And when he is come, he will reprove the world of sin, and of righteousness, and of judgment: of sin, because they believe not on me; of righteousness, because I go to my Father, and ye see me no more; of judgment, because the prince of this world is judged."—John 16:8–11.

~

THE Apostles had a stern task before them. They were to go into all nations and proclaim the gospel to every creature, beginning at Jerusalem. Remember that only two or three years before they were simple fishermen engaged upon the Galilean lake—men of little or no education, men of no rank or standing. At best they were but Jews, and that nation was everywhere despised, while these peasants were not even men of repute among their own nation. Yet these men were to turn the world upside down. They were told by their Lord that they would be brought before rulers and kings for his sake, and that they would be persecuted wherever they went. They were to proclaim the gospel in the teeth of the imperial power of Rome, the ancient wisdom of Greece, and the fierce cruelties of barbaric lands, and to set up the kingdom of peace and righteousness.

At the very time when they were about to receive their commission, they were also to lose the bodily presence of their great Leader. While he was with them they had felt no fear. If they were puzzled at any time by the Scribes and Pharisees, they resorted to Jesus, and they were rescued from bewilderment. Never man spoke like that man; never did such wisdom and prudence dwell in any mind as dwelt in the mind of Christ. His presence was their ægis, the broad shield behind which they stood securely, whatever shafts might be shot at them by their adversaries. But now that he was to depart out of the world unto the Father they would be deprived of their fortress and high tower; they would be as children bereft of their father, or, at best, as soldiers without a general. Here was a sad case. Work given, and power withdrawn: a battle beginning, and the conquering captain leaving.

How happy was it for these disciples that our blessed Lord could tell them that his going away would be for their gain rather than for their loss; for when he was gone the Spirit of God would come to be an advocate for them and with them, and by his power they would be able to silence all their enemies and achieve their mission. The Holy Spirit was to be their Comforter, that they might not be afraid, and their Advocate, that they might not be baffled. When they spoke, there would be a power within them suggesting their words, a power with those words convincing their hearers, and a power in their hearers causing the word spoken to abide in their memories: that power would be divine, the power of the Holy Ghost, who is one God with the Father and the Son. It is one thing for men to speak, and quite another thing for God to speak through men. The work of proclaiming the gospel to the world was far too great for the twelve; but it was by no means too great for the Spirit of God. Who can limit his power? Is anything too hard for the Lord? The Holy Spirit being their helper, these feeble men were equal to the task which God had committed to their trust. The presence of the Holy Ghost was better for them than the bodily presence of the Lord Jesus. The Lord Jesus could only have been in one place as to his corporeal presence, but the Holy Ghost could be everywhere; the sight of Jesus would but appeal to the senses, but the power of the Holy Ghost touched the heart and wrought spiritual life and saving faith; thus, by his own withdrawal and the sending of the Spirit, our Lord furnished his servants for the conflict.

We will at this time observe what the Holy Spirit did as an Advocate. The passage cannot be fully understood except we give it three renderings; and I do not pretend that even then we shall have pressed from this choice cluster all the generous wine of its meaning. To my mind, it is a compendium of all the work of the Spirit of God. By our three readings we shall see much: first, the Spirit of God goes with the preaching of the gospel to *reprove* men of sin, and so to abash them in the presence of the preacher of righteousness; secondly (and this is a much more blessed result), to *convince* men of sin, and so to lead them to repentance towards God and faith in our Lord Jesus Christ; and, thirdly, the ultimate result of the Holy Spirit's work will be to *convict* men before all intelligent beings of having been guilty of the grossest sin, of having opposed the most perfect righteousness, and of having defied the most glorious judgment. We shall try to see the meaning of the passage through these three windows.

I. First, we believe that a promise is here made to the servants of Christ, that when they go forth to preach the gospel the Holy Ghost will be with them TO REPROVE MEN. By this is meant, not so much to save them as to silence them. When the minister of Christ stands up to plead his Master's cause, another advocate appears in court, whose pleadings would make it hard for men to resist the truth.

Observe how this reproof was given with regard to *sin*.

On the day of Pentecost the disciples spoke with divers tongues, as the Spirit gave them utterance. Men from all countries under heaven heard themselves addressed in their native tongues. This was a great marvel, and all Jerusalem rang with it; and when Peter stood up to preach to the assembled multitude, and told the Jews that they had crucified the Holy One and the Just, the signs and wonders wrought by the Spirit in the name of Jesus were a witness which they could not refute. The very fact that the Spirit of God had given to these unlettered men the gift of tongues was evidence that Jesus of Nazareth, of whom they spoke, was no impostor. It was laid down in the old Jewish law, that if a man prophesied and his prophecies did not come to pass, he was to be condemned as a false prophet; but if that which he said came to pass, then he was a true prophet. Now, the Lord Jesus Christ had promised the outpouring of the Spirit, which had also been foretold in reference to the Messiah by the prophet Joel; when, therefore, that mark of the true Messiah was set upon Jesus of Nazareth by the coming of the Holy Spirit and the working of miracles, men were reproved for having refused to believe in Jesus. The evidence was brought home to them that they had with wicked hands crucified the Lord of glory: and so they stood reproved.

All the subsequent miracles went to prove the same thing; for when the apostles wrought miracles the world was reproved of sin because it believed not on Christ. It was not that a few disciples testified to the sin of the race, but the Holy Spirit himself made men tremble as by his deeds of power he bore witness to the Lord Jesus, and exhibited the fact that in crucifying him the world had put to death the incarnate Son of God. Do you not see the terrible power with which the first disciples were thus armed? It was more to them than the rod in the hand of Moses with which he smote Pharaoh with so many plagues. It needed all the wilfulness of that stiff-necked generation to resist the Holy Spirit and refuse to bow before him whom they had pierced; they were full of malice and obstinacy, but in their secret hearts they were sore put to it, and felt that they were fighting against God.

Do you not see, too, dear friends, how the working of the Holy Spirit with the apostles and their immediate followers was a wonderful rebuke to the world concerning the matter of *righteousness*. Jesus was gone, and his divine example no longer stood out like clear light reproving their darkness, but the Holy Spirit attested that righteousness, and compelled them to feel that Jesus was the Holy One, and that his cause was righteous. The teaching of the apostles, sealed by the Holy Spirit, made the world see what righteousness was as they had never seen it before. A fresh standard of morals was set up in the world, and it has never been taken down: it stands in its place to rebuke, if not to improve. The world was then sunken in the uttermost depths of vice, and even its good men were loathsome; but now another kind of righteousness was exhibited in the teachings of the Lord Jesus, and the Spirit came to set the seal of divine approval thereto, so that if men continued in sin it might be against light and knowledge, for they now knew what was righteousness, and could no longer mistake upon that point. God was with the preachers of a new righteousness, and by divers signs and wonders he attested the cause of the gospel Now, brethren, we also rejoice in this, seeing that the witness of truth is for all time, and we know of a surety that the kingdom which our Lord Jesus has set up among men is divinely sanctioned as the kingdom of righteousness, which in the end shall grind to powder the powers of evil. We are the covenanted servants of a Lord whose righteousness was declared among men by the personal witness of God the Holy Ghost. Are you not glad to be enlisted in such a service? Oh, world! art thou not reproved for resisting such a kingdom?

These twelve fishermen could not of themselves have exhibited a new standard of righteousness among men;

they could not on their own account have set before all nations a higher ideal of moral excellence; but when the eternal power and majesty of the Godhead vouched for the righteousness of the Lord Jesus, the course of the apostolic church became like that of the sun in the heavens. "Their line is gone out through all the earth, and their words to the end of the world." None could stand against them; for, as when the morning breaks the darkness flies and the bats and the night-birds hasten away, so when the messengers of mercy proclaimed the righteousness of God, man's hypocrisy and self-glorying fled away.

Then, too, they were made to feel that a *judgment* had come; that somehow the life and the death of Jesus of Nazareth had made a crisis in the world's history, and condemned the way and manner of the ungodly. All historians must confess that the turning point of the race is the cross of Christ. It would be impossible to fix any other hinge of history. From that moment the power of evil received its mortal wound. It dies hard, but from that hour it was doomed. At the death of our Lord the heathen oracles were struck dumb. There had been oracles all over the world, either the product of evil spirits or of crafty priests; but after the Christian era the world ceased to believe in these voices, and they were no more heard. Systems of false worship, so firmly rooted in prejudice and custom that it seemed impossible that they should ever be overthrown, were torn up by their roots by the breath of the Lord. The apostles might have said to all the systems of falsehood, "as a bowing wall shall ye be, and as a tottering fence." Men could not help perceiving that the prince of darkness had been cast down from his undivided power, and that he spake henceforth with bated breath. The seed of the woman had met the old serpent, and in the duel between them he had gained such a victory that the cause of evil was henceforth hopeless.

Moreover, the thought flashed upon humanity more

clearly than ever it had done before—that there would be a day of judgment. Men heard and felt the truth of the warning that God would judge the world at the last by the man Christ Jesus. The dim forms of Rhadamanthus on a cloudy judgment seat, and of the assembly before his throne, and of the crowds divided according to their lives, now began to assume another and far more definite shape. It was written on the heart of mankind that there is a judgment to come! Men will rise again; they shall stand before the judgment-seat of Christ to give an account of the things done in the body, whether good or evil. The world heard this, and the tidings have never been forgotten. The Holy Ghost has reproved men by the prospect of judgment.

The Holy Spirit attested the life of Christ, the teaching of the apostles, and all the grand truths that were contained therein, by what he did in the way of miracle, and by what he did in the way of enlightening, impressing, and subduing human hearts. Henceforth man is accused, and rebuked by the great Advocate; and all who remain in opposition to the Lord Jesus, remain so in defiance of the clearest proofs of his mission. He who rejects human testimony when it is true is foolish; but he who despises the witness of the Holy Ghost is profane, for he gives the lie to the Spirit of truth. Let him beware lest he so sin against the Holy Ghost as to come under the most terrible of curses; for it is written of him that speaketh against the Holy Ghost, "he hath never forgiveness."

Brethren, does not that put the apostles in quite a different position from that in which they appeared to be? If we judge according to sense and carnal reason, their adventure was Quixotic, their success was impossible. Everybody would have said to them, "Go back to your nets and to your boats. What can you do against the established system of Judaism in your own country? And if that be too hard for you, what will you be able to do in other lands? There are nations that have been tutored in their own learning for thousands of years, and have become adepts in all the arts and sciences; they have brought all the charms of poetry, and music, and statuary, to support their idolatrous systems: you are fools to think that you unlearned and ignorant men can ever overturn all this." Would not prudence agree with this? Ay, but if God is in these men, if he that dwelt in the bush at Horeb, and made it burn, though it was not consumed, will dwell in them, and each one of them shall be gifted with a tongue of fire, this is a different business altogether. Surely, he that made the world, could new-make it. He that said, "Let there be light, and there was light," could command light to shine upon the moral and spiritual night.

Thus much upon the first reading of the text. Let us advance to that which will more interest you.

II. The Holy Spirit was to go with the preaching of the word TO CONVINCE MEN of three great prominent truths. This was to be a saving word: they are to be so convinced as to repent of sin, to accept of righteousness, and yield themselves to the judgment of the Lord. Here we see as in a map the work of the Spirit upon the hearts of those who are ordained unto eternal life. Those three effects are all necessary, and each one is in the highest degree important to true conversion.

First, the Holy Ghost is come to convince men of *sin*. It is absolutely necessary that men should be convinced of sin. The fashionable theology is—"Convince men of the goodness of God: show them the universal fatherhood and assure them of unlimited mercy. Win them by God's love, but never mention his wrath against sin, or the need of an atonement, or the possibility of there being a place of punishment. Do not censure poor creatures for their failings. Do not judge and condemn. Do not search the heart or lead men to be low-spirited and sorrowful. Comfort and encourage, but never accuse and threaten." Yes, that is the way of man; but the way of the Spirit of God is very different. He comes on purpose to convince men of sin, to make them feel that they are guilty, greatly guilty—so guilty that they are lost, and ruined, and undone. He comes to remind them not only of God's loveliness, but of their own unloveliness; of their own enmity and hatred to this God of love, and, consequently, of their terrible sin in thus ill-using one so infinitely kind. The Holy Ghost does not come to make sinners comfortable in their sins, but to cause them to grieve over their sins. He does not help them to forget their sin, or think little of it, but he comes to convince them of the horrible enormity of their iniquity. It is no work of the Spirit to pipe to men's dancing: he does not bring forth flute, harp, dulcimer, and all kinds of music to charm the unbelieving into a good opinion of themselves; but he comes to make sin appear sin, and to let us see its fearful consequences. He comes to wound so that no human balm can heal: to kill so that no earthly power can make us live. The flowers bedeck the meadows when the grass is green; but lo! a burning wind comes from the desert, and the grass withereth, and the flower thereof falleth away. What is it that makes the beauty and excellence of human righteousness to wither as the green herb? Isaiah says it is "because the Spirit of the Lord bloweth upon it." There is a withering work of the Spirit of God which we must experience, or we shall never know his quickening and restoring power. This withering is a most needful experience, and just now needs much to be insisted on. To-day we have so many built up who were never pulled down; so many filled who were never emptied; so many exalted who were never humbled; that I the more earnestly remind you that the Holy Ghost must convince us of sin, or we cannot be saved.

This work is most necessary, because without it there is no leading men to receive the gospel of the grace of God. We cannot make headway with certain people because they profess faith very readily, but they are not convinced of anything. "Oh, yes, we are sinners, no doubt, and Christ died for sinners": that is the free-and-easy way with which they handle heavenly mysteries, as if they were the nonsense verses of a boy's exercise, or the stories of Mother Goose. This is all mockery, and we are weary of it. But get near a real sinner, and you have found a man you can deal with: I mean the man who is a sinner, and no mistake, and mourns in his inmost soul that he is so. In such a man you find one who will welcome the gospel, welcome grace, and welcome a Saviour. To him the news of pardon will be as cold water to a thirsty soul, and the doctrine of grace will be as honey dropping from the comb. "A sinner," says one of our songsters, "is a sacred thing: the Holy Ghost hath made him so." Your sham sinner is a horrid creature; but a man truly convinced of sin by the Spirit of God is a being to be sought after as a jewel that will adorn the crown of the Redeemer.

Note here, that the Spirit of God comes to convince men of sin, because they never will be convinced of sin apart from his divine advocacy. A natural conscience touched by the Spirit of God may do a good deal in the way of showing a man his faults; it may thus make him uneasy, and may bring about a reformation of life; but it is only the Spirit of God that to the full extent convinces a man of sin so as to bring forth repentance, self-despair, and faith in Jesus. For what is the sin that you and I are guilty of? Ah, brethren, it were not easy to tell; but this I know, that the extent of sin is never known till the Spirit of God reveals the secret chambers of the heart's abominations. We do a thousand things that we do not know to be sin till the Spirit of God enlightens us and pleads the cause of holiness in us. What natural man, for instance, ever laments over evil thoughts or desires, or the imaginations which flit across his mind? Yet all these are sins, and sins which cause a gracious heart the deepest distress. If we were never actually to commit evil, yet if we desire to do so, we have already sinned; and if we feel pleasure in thinking of evil, we have already sinned. This poison is in our nature, and shows itself in a thousand ways. The fact that we not only sin, but are by nature sinful, is one which our pride kicks against, and we will not learn it till the Spirit of God teaches it to us. Neither does any man know the exceeding sinfulness of sin till the light falls upon the black mass from the Holy Spirit. Every sin is, as it were, an assault upon God's throne, glory, and life. Sin would dethrone the Most High, and destroy him if it could; but men do not see this. They talk of sin most lightly, and know not that it scatters firebrands and death. I tell you, when the Spirit of God makes a man see sin in its naked deformity, he is horrified. When I saw, or thought I saw, the heinousness of sin, it was intolerable, and I had no rest in my spirit. Some such a sight we must all have, or we shall never look to the Lord Jesus to take away our sin. None but those whose wounds smart are likely to apply for the heavenly balm.

The Holy Spirit dwells upon one point in particular: "of sin, because they believe not on me." None see the sin of unbelief except by his light. For a man thinks, "Well, if I have not believed in Christ, that is a pity, perhaps; but still, I was never a thief, or a liar, or a drunkard, or unchaste. Unbelief is a matter of very little consequence; I can set that square at any time." But the Holy Spirit makes a man see that not to believe in Christ is a crowning, damning sin, since he that believeth not hath made God a liar: and what can be more atrocious than that? He who believes not on Christ has rejected God's mercy, and has done despite to the grandest display of God's love; he hath despised God's unspeakable gift, and trampled on the blood of Christ. In this he has dishonoured God on a very tender point; has insulted him concerning his only-begotten Son. How I wish that the Spirit of God would come upon unbelievers here, and make them see what they are and where they are with regard to the one and only Saviour. How shall they escape who neglect so great salvation? It will not matter how feebly I speak this morning if the Spirit of God will only work by the truth, you will perceive the greatness of your crime, and you will never rest until you have believed on the Lord Jesus, and found forgiveness for your high offence against the bleeding Lamb. So far, then, upon the first operation of the Holy Ghost.

The next work of the Spirit is to convince men of *righteousness;* that is to say, in gospel terms, to show them that they have no righteousness of their own, and no means of working righteousness, and that apart from grace they are condemned. Thus he leads them to value the righteousness of God which is upon all them that believe, even a righteousness which covers sin, and renders them acceptable with God.

Lend me your ears a moment while I call your attention to a great wonder. Among men, if a person is convicted of wrong-doing, the next step is judgment. A young man, for instance, has been in the service of an employer, and he has embezzled money: he is convicted of the theft by process of law, and found guilty. What follows next? Why, judgment is pronounced, and he must suffer penalty. But observe how our gracious God interpolates another process. Truly, his ways are not our ways! "He shall convince of sin ——" The next step would be judgment; but no, the Lord inserts a hitherto unknown middle term, and convinces "of righteousness." Be amazed at this. The Lord takes a man, even when he is sinful and conscious of that sin, and makes him righteous on the spot, by putting away his sin and justifying him by the righteousness of faith, a righteousness which comes to him by the worthiness of another who has wrought out a righteousness for him. Can that be? Brethren, this seems to be a thing so impossible that it needs the Spirit of God to convince men of it. I may now set forth the great plan whereby the Lord Jesus is made of God unto us righteousness; I may show how the Son of God became man that he might fully keep the law of God for us, and that having done so, and having added his passive obedience to his active service, he presented to his Father a complete vindication of his injured law, so that every man that believeth on him shall be delivered from condemnation, and accepted in the Beloved. I might also tell how Christ's righteousness is set to our account, so that faith is reckoned unto us for righteousness, even as was the case with faithful Abraham. Yet all my labour will be in vain till the Spirit shall make it plain. Many hear the gladsome tidings; but they do not receive the truth, for they are not convinced of it. They need to be persuaded of it before they will embrace it; and that persuasion is not in my power. Did I hear one remark, "I cannot see this way of righteousness"? I answer, No, and you never will until the Spirit of God convinces you of it.

Note well the great point of the Spirit's argument,— "Of righteousness, because I go to my Father, and ye see me no more." Our Lord was sent into the world to work out a righteousness, and bere he says "I go"; but he would not go till he had done his work. He says also, "I go to my Father"; but he would not go back to his Father till he had fulfilled his covenant engagements. "I go to my Father"; that is, I go to receive a reward and to sit upon my Father's throne; and he could not have received this glory if he had not finished his appointed work. Behold, then, Christ has finished a righteousness which is freely given to all them that believe, and all those who trust in Christ are for his sake regarded as righteous before God, and are in fact righteous, so that Paul saith, "Who is he that condemneth?" His ground for asking that question is the same as that which the Spirit uses in my text. He says, "It is Christ that died, yea rather, that is risen again, who is even at the right hand of God, who also maketh intercession for us." He quotes, as the Holy Spirit does, the resurrection, ascension, and enthronement of the great Intercessor as the proof positive that there is a perfect righteousness for all believing sinners. I know that many will say, "This is making people righteous who are not righteous," and hence they will raise many objections. Just so! This is the glory of God, that he justifieth the ungodly, and saves sinners by Christ. "Blessed is the man unto whom the Lord imputeth not iniquity." "I do not see it," cries one. And our answer is, "We know you do not: we are not in the least surprised that you reject our testimony; we never expected you to receive it unless the arm of the Lord should be revealed, and the Holy Ghost should convince you of righteousness." No man comes to Christ who is not drawn of the Father and enlightened by the Spirit; but if the Spirit convinces you we shall soon hear you sing—

"Jesus, thy blood and righteousness
My beauty are, my glorious dress;
Midst flaming worlds, in these arrayed,
With joy shall I lift up my head."

Dear people of God, pray hard that the Spirit of God may even now convince unbelievers that the only true righteousness for mortal men is that which comes not by the works of the law, but by the hearing of faith.

But then comes a third point, the Spirit of God is to convince men *of judgment*. To whom is this judgment committed? "The Father hath committed all judgment unto the Son." The true penitent feels that if he had all his sins forgiven him yet it will not serve his turn so long as he lies wallowing in sin. He feels that the great enemy of his soul must be dethroned, or else forgiveness itself will afford him no rest of heart. He must be rescued from the power as well as from the guilt of sin, or else he abides in bondage. He must see the power of evil hewn in pieces before the Lord as Samuel hewed Agag of old. Hearken, O troubled one! You shall be set free, for "the prince of this world is judged." Jesus came to destroy the works of the devil; and on the cross our Redeemer judged Satan, overcame him, and cast him down. He is now a condemned criminal, a vanquished rebel. His reigning power over all believers is broken. He hath great wrath, knowing that his time is short, but that wrath is held in check by his conqueror. In his passion our Lord fought Satan foot to foot, and overcame him, spoiling principalities and powers, and making a show of them openly, triumphing over them in it. Believest thou this? May the Spirit of God convince you of it! O tried believer, the Lord Jesus overthrew the devil for you. He crushed the powers of darkness for you; and believing in him you shall find evil dethroned in you, and all the forces of sin hurled from their high places. You shall overcome through the blood of the Lamb. Again I say, believest thou this? Christ is made of God unto us sanctification; he saves his people from their sins; he makes them holy, and so breaks in pieces their enemy. Though it will cost you many a conflict, and the beaded sweat may in the hour of temptation stand upon your brow, as you fear that you will fall from holiness, yet the Lord shall bruise Satan under your feet shortly, for he has already bruised him under his own feet on your behalf. The Spirit of God is needed to convince our unbelieving hearts that it is even so. Most men dream that they must overcome sin by their own strength. Alas, the strong man armed still keeps the house against our feebleness. You have a pretty piece of work before you if in your own strength you venture on this conflict. I can hear the devil laughing at you even now. This leviathan is not to be tamed by you. Job would say, "Wilt thou play with him as with a bird?" Dost thou think the devil is as easily managed as a woman carries her pet bird on her finger, and puts it to her lip to peck a seed? Canst thou draw out leviathan with a hook? Will he speak soft words unto thee? Wilt thou take him to be a servant for ever? Thine arrows cannot come at him, nor thy sword wound him. "Lay thine hand upon him, remember the battle, do no more." A power divine is needed, and that power is ready to display itself if it be humbly sought.

Many who are convinced of the righteousness of

Christ are not yet fully convinced that evil is judged, and condemned, and cast down. They are haunted with the dread that they may yet perish by the hand of the enemy. Oh, my brother, see the need of the Holy Spirit to advocate in thy heart the cause of God and truth, and make thee believe that the Lord Jesus hath supreme power over every enemy. I sometimes meet with a Christian brother who tells me the world is all going to the bad, the gospel is being utterly defeated, Christ is routed, the devil is waving the black flag and shouting victory. I know how terrible is the conflict, but I believe that my Lord Jesus has judged the whole kingdom of evil, and in that fact I see Satan fall like lightning from heaven. Our Lord *must* reign. His enemies must lick the dust. We shall judge the fallen angels at the last great day, and meanwhile a believing life is a life of triumph over the arch enemy. In the power of the Spirit it shall be proven that truth is mightier than error, love is stronger than hate, and holiness is higher than sin; for the Lord's right hand and his holy arm have gotten him the victory. Behold how the ascended Saviour leads captivity captive. See how he comes from Edom, with dyed garments from Bozrah, for he has trodden sin and hell in the winepress, and now he travelleth in the greatness of his strength, speaking in righteousness, mighty to save.

Let me run again over this ground, that we may not overlook anything. Dear friends, those of us who are saved still need the Holy Spirit with us every day to convince us of sin. Good men do at this hour most complacently things which in clearer light they will never think of doing. May the Holy Spirit continually show us layer after layer of sin, that we may remove it; may he reveal to us rank after rank of sin, that we may conquer all its forces. May he especially discover to us the sin of not believing in Christ, for even we have our doubts and fears. After a sermon concerning sin the poor child of God cries out, "I dare not believe. I am afraid I shall be lost after all." This unbelief is another sin. Strange way of escaping from sin by plunging into it! To doubt the Lord is to add sin to sin. No sin is more pernicious than the sin of not believing. Whenever our heart distrusts the Lord we grieve his Spirit; hence we always need the Holy Ghost to convince us of this evil and bitter thing, and to lead us to trust after a childlike fashion. Any mistrust of God's promise, any fear of failure on God's part, any thought of his unfaithfulness, is a crime against the honour of the divine majesty. Oh, convincing Spirit, dwell with me from day to day convincing me of sin, and especially making me to feel that the worst of all evils is to question my faithful Friend.

So, also, may you always have the Spirit of God dwelling with you, convincing you of righteousness. May those of you who are indeed believers never question but what you are righteous before God. We who believe are made the righteousness of God in Christ Jesus: are we assured of this? If so, do not think and talk as if you were still under the curse of the law, for you are no longer in any such condition. "Therefore being justified by faith, we have peace with God through our Lord Jesus Christ." "There is therefore now no condemnation to them which are in Christ Jesus." Oh, may the Spirit of God every day convince you of that; and convince you of it on the ground that Jesus is reigning yonder at the Father's right hand. The interest of each believer in his Lord is clear and sure. If Jesus is there, I am there. If the Father has accepted him, he has accepted me. Do you catch the logic of it? You are in Christ, you are one with him: as he is so are you in him. Do hold fast to the fact that you are not condemned. How can you be? You are at the right hand of God in Christ. You condemned! Why, you are "accepted in the Beloved," for your representative is accepted by God and made to sit upon his throne. Jesus is exalted, not for himself alone, but for all those who believe in him. May the blessed Spirit fully convince you of this grand truth.

And, next, may he convince you of judgment—

namely, that you have been judged, and your enemy has been judged, and condemned. The day of judgment is not a thing to be dreaded by a believer. We have stood our trial, and have been acquitted. Our representative has borne the penalty of our sin. Our chastisement is passed: for Jesus has borne it: he was numbered with transgressors. There is now no curse for us: there can be none: heaven, earth, hell cannot find a curse for those whom God has blessed, since the Lord Jesus "was made a curse for us." May the Spirit of God come on you afresh, my dearly beloved, and make you confident and joyful in him who is the Lord our righteousness, by whom evil has been judged once for all!

III. Last of all, let us read our text by rendering it "convict"—"The Spirit of God will CONVICT the world of sin, of righteousness, and of judgment." There is the world. It stands a prisoner at the bar, and the charge is that it is and has been full of sin. In courts of law you are often surprised with what comes out. You look at the prisoner, and he seems to be a quiet, respectable person, and you say, "I should not think he is guilty." But the advocate who has engaged to plead the cause of righteousness stands up and gives an outline of the case; and you speedily change your mind, until as the evidence proceeds you say to yourself, "That is a villain, if ever there was one." Now hear the Spirit of God. The Spirit came into the world to make all men know that Jesus is the Christ, and he attested that fact by miracles that could not be questioned, miracles without number: he has moreover attested the truth of the gospel by the conversion of myriads, whose happy and holy lives have been a proof that Jesus Christ was indeed sent forth from God. But what did this wicked world do with Christ? They gave him a felon's death: they nailed him to a cross. By this the world is condemned! We need no further evidence. The world is convicted: self-condemned by the slaughter of him who was incarnate goodness and unbounded love. The world is base enough to desire to slay its God even when he comes on an errand of love. Take the accused away! The world's guilt is proven beyond question. The wrath of God abideth on it.

What follows upon this? The trial is viewed from another point. The world has declared that the gospel is not righteous, that the system which our Lord has come to establish is not true. Up to this day the world is continually raising objections, trying to confound believers, and, if possible, to defeat our most holy cause. But the Spirit of God by his teaching proves that the gospel is full of righteousness; and by all his operations through the word he proves that the gospel is holy, and just, and good, and tends to make men pure, godly, peaceable, and holy. By sanctifying men through the gospel so that they lead gracious lives, the Holy Spirit proves that the gospel is righteous. This process grows more and more complete as time rolls on. Were not the world unrighteous it would long ago have yielded to the holy message and its holy Messenger. But it will be forced to own the truth one day. The Holy Spirit makes the world know that Christ is righteous by flashing into its face the fact that Christ has gone,—gone up to glory, at the right hand of God,—and this could not have been had he not been the righteous One.

When the world shall see Jesus enthroned at the last, and all mankind shall behold the Son of man on the clouds of heaven, what conviction will seize on every mind! There will be no agnostics then! Not a sceptic will be found in that day! Christ seen at the Father's right hand will end all unbelief!

And then the Spirit of God shall make men see the judgment. Before the day actually comes, they shall perceive that since Christ has judged the devil, since Christ has cast him down from his high places, and his power over the world is already broken, assuredly he will smite all that are in the dominion of Satan, and will not allow one of them to escape. The cause of evil is judged, and its case is desperate. Oh, how the Spirit of God will convict men at that last day when they hear the Judge say, "Come, ye blessed of my Father," or "Depart, ye cursed, into everlasting fire."

Men and brethren, will you be convinced by the Holy Spirit now, or will you wait till then? Shall it be the convincement of grace or the conviction of wrath? The Spirit bears witness still with us who preach the gospel: will you yield to that gospel, and believe it now? or will you wait until the blaze of the last tremendous day? Which shall it be? I think I hear you say, "The gospel is true." Why, then, do you not believe it? If you confess "sin," why are you not washed from it? If there be "righteousness," why do you not seek it? If there be "judgment," why do you not ask to be so cleansed that you need not be afraid of it? Oh, sirs, the most of men act as if they were born fools. If they were sick, and we had a sure medicine for them, they would rush to us for it. If they were poor, and we brought them gold, they would tread us down in their vehemence to snatch at wealth. But when there is Christ to be had, the divine remedy for sin, Christ to be had as a perfect righteousness, Christ to make them stand securely at the last dread day, they turn their backs upon the heavenly boon. Oh, Spirit of God, win these madmen; bring back these fools and make them sane and wise, for Christ Jesus' sake. Amen.

8
THE HOLY GHOST—THE GREAT TEACHER

"Howbeit when he, the Spirit of truth, is come, he will guide you into all truth: for he, shall not speak of himself; but whatsoever he shall hear, that shall he speak: and he will shew you things to come."—John 16:13.

~

THIS generation hath gradually, and almost imperceptibly, become to a great extent a godless generation. One of the diseases of the present generation of mankind, is their secret but deep-seated godlessness, by which they have so far departed from the knowledge of God. Science has discovered to us second causes; and hence, many have too much forgotten the first Great Cause, the Author of all: they have been able so far to pry into secrets, that the great axiom of the existence of a God, has been too much neglected. Even among professing Christians, while there is a great amount of religion, there is too, little godliness: there is much external formalism, but too little inward acknowledgment of God, too little living on God, living with God, and relying upon God. Hence arises the sad fact, that when you enter many of our places of worship you will certainly hear the name of God mentioned; but except in the benediction, you would scarcely know there was a Trinity. In many places dedicated to Jehovah the name of Jesus is too often kept in the background; the Holy Spirit is almost entirely neglected; and very little is said concerning his sacred influence. Even religious men have become to a large degree godless in this age. We sadly require more preaching regarding God; more preaching of those things which look not so much at the creature to be saved, as at God the Great One to be extolled. My firm conviction is, that in proportion as we have more regard for the sacred godhead, the wondrous Trinity in Unity, shall we see a greater display of God's power, and a more glorious manifestation of his might in our churches. May God send us a Christ-exalting. Spirit-loving ministry—men who shall proclaim God the Holy Ghost in all his offices, and shall extol God the Saviour as the author and finisher of our faith; not neglecting that Great God, the Father of his people, who, before all worlds, elected us in Christ his Son, justified us through his righteousness, and will inevitably preserve us and gather us together in one, in the consummation of all things at the last great day.

Our text has regard to God the Holy Spirit; of Him we shall speak and Him only, if His sweet influence shall rest upon us.

The disciples had been instructed by Christ concerning certain elementary doctrines, but Jesus did not teach his disciples more than what we should call the A B C of religion. He gives his reasons for this in the 12th verse: "I have yet many things to say unto you, but you cannot bear them now." His disciples were not possessors of the Spirit. They had the Spirit so far as the work of conversion was concerned, but not as to the matters of bright illumination, profound instruction, prophecy, and inspiration. He says, "I am now about to depart, and when I go from you I will send the Comforter unto you. Ye cannot bear these things now, howbeit, when he, the Spirit of truth is come, he will guide you into all truth." The same promise that he made to his apostles, stands good to all his children; and in reviewing it, we shall take it as *our* portion and heritage, and shall not consider ourselves intruders upon the manor of the apostles, or upon their exclusive rights and prerogatives; for we conceive that Jesus says even to us, "When he, the Spirit of truth is come, he will guide you into all truth."

Dwelling exclusively upon our text, we have five things. First of all, here is *an attainment mentioned*—a knowledge of all truth; secondly, here is *a difficulty suggested*—which is, that we need guidance into all truth; thirdly, here is *a person provided*—"when he, the Spirit shall come, he shall guide you into all truth;" fourthly, here is *a manner hinted at*—"he shall guide you into all truth;" fifthly here is *a sign given as to the working of the Spirit*—we may know whether he works, by his "guiding us into *all* truth,"—into all of one thing; not *truths*, but *truth*.

I. Here is AN ATTAINMENT MENTIONED, which is a knowledge of all truth. We know that some conceive doctrinal knowledge to be of very little importance, and of no practical use. We do not think so. We believe the science of Christ crucified and a judgment of the teachings of Scripture to be exceedingly valuable; we think it is right, that the Christian ministry should not only be arousing but instructing; not merely awakening, but enlightening; that it should appeal not only to the passions but to the understanding. We are far from thinking doctrinal knowledge to be of secondary importance; we believe it to be one of the first things in the Christian life, to know the truth, and then to practise it. We scarcely need this morning tell you how desirable it is for us to be well taught in things of the kingdom

First of all, *nature itself*, (when it has been sanctified by grace,) *gives us a strong desire to know all truth*. The natural man separateth himself and intermeddleth with all knowledge. God has put an instinct in him by which he is rendered unsatisfied if he cannot probe mystery to its bottom; he can never be content until he can unriddle secrets. What we call curiosity is something given us of God impelling us to search into the knowledge of natural things; that curiosity, sanctified by the Spirit, is also brought to bear in matters of heavenly science and celestial wisdom. "Bless the Lord," said David, "O my soul, and *all that is within me* bless his holy name!" If there is a curiosity within us, it ought to be employed and developed in a search after truth. "All that is within me," sanctified by the Spirit should be developed. And, verily, the Christian man feels an intense longing to bury his ignorance and receive wisdom. If he, when in his natural estate panted for terrestrial knowledge, how much more ardent is the wish to unravel, if possible, the sacred mysteries of God's Word! A true Christian is always intently reading and searching the Scripture that he may be able to certify himself as to its main and cardinal truths. I do not think much of that man who does not wish to understand doctrines; I cannot conceive him to be in a right position when he thinks it is no matter whether he believes a lie or truth, whether he is heretic or orthodox, whether he received the Word of God as it is written, or as it is diluted and misconstrued by man. God's Word will ever be to a Christian a source of great anxiety; a sacred instinct within will lead him to pry into it; he will seek to understand it. Oh! there are some who forget this, men who purposely abstain from mentioning what are called high doctrines, because they think if they should mention high doctrines they would be dangerous; so they keep them back. Foolish men! they do not know anything of human nature; for if they did understand a grain's worth of humanity, they would know that the hiding of these things impels men to search them out. From the fact that they do not mention them, they drive men to places where these, and these only, are preached. They say, "If I preach election, and predestination, and these dark things, people will all go straight away, and become Antinomians." I am not so sure if they were to be called Antinomians it would hurt them much; but hear me, oh, ye ministers that conceal these truths, that is the way to make them Antinomians, by silencing these doctrines. Curiosity is strong; if you tell them they must not pluck the truth, they will be sure to do it; but if you give it to them as you find it in God's Word, they will not seek to "wrest" it. Enlightened men *will* have the truth; and if they see election in Scripture they will say, "*it is there*, and I will find it out. If I cannot get it in one place, I will get it in another." The true Christian has an inward longing and anxiety after it; he is hungry and thirsty after the word of righteousness, and he must and will feed on this bread of heaven, or at all hazards he will leave the husks which unsound divines would offer him.

Not only is this attainment to be desired because nature teaches us so, but a knowledge of all truth is *very essential for our comfort*. I do believe that many persons have been distressed half their lives from the fact that they had not clear views of truth. Many poor souls, for instance, under conviction, abide three or four times as long in sorrow of mind as they would require to do if they had some one to instruct them in the great matter of justification. So there are believers who are often troubling themselves about falling away; but if they knew in their soul the great consolation that we are kept by the grace of God through faith unto salvation, they would be no more troubled about it. So have I found some distressed about the unpardonable sin; but if God instructs us in that doctrine, and shows us that no conscience that is really awakened ever can commit that sin, but that when it is committed God gives us up to a seared conscience, so that we never fear or tremble afterwards, all that distress would be alleviated. Depend on this, the more you know of God's truth—all things else being equal—the more comfortable you will be as a Christian. Nothing can give a greater light on your path than a clear understanding of divine things. It is a mingle-mangled gospel too commonly preached, which causes the downcast faces of Christians. Give me the congregation whose faces are bright with joy, let their eyes glisten at the sound of the gospel, then will I believe that it is God's own words they are receiving. Instead thereof you will often see melancholy congregations whose visages are not much different from the bitter countenance of poor creatures swallowing medicine, because the word spoken terrifies them by its legality, instead of comforting them by its grace. We love a cheerful gospel, and we think "all the truth" will tend to comfort the Christian.

"Comfort again?" says another, "always comfort." Ah, but there is another reason why we prize truth, because we believe that a true knowledge of all the truth *will keep us very much out of danger*. No doctrine is so calculated to preserve a man from sin as the doctrine of the grace of God. Those who have called it a licentious doctrine did not know anything at all about it. Poor ignorant things, they little knew that their own vile stuff was the most licentious doctrine under heaven. If they knew the grace of God in truth, they would soon see that there was no preservative from lying like a knowlege that we are elect of God from the foundation of the world. There is nothing like a belief in my eternal perseverance, and the immutability of my Father's affection, which can keep me near to him from a motive of simple gratitude. Nothing makes a man so virtuous as belief of truth. A lying doctrine will soon beget a lying practice. A man cannot have an erroneous belief without by-and-bye having an erroneous life. I believe the one thing naturally begets the other. Keep near God's truth; keep near his word: keep the head right, and especially keep your heart right with regard to truth, and your feet will not go for astray.

Again, I hold also that this attainment to the knowledge of all truth is very desirable for *the usefulness which it will give us in the world at large*. We should not be selfish: we should always consider whether a thing will be beneficial to others. A knowledge of all truth will make us very serviceable in this world. We shall be skilful physicians who know how to take the poor distressed soul aside, to put the finger on his eye, and take the scale off for him, that heaven's light may comfort him. There will be no character, however perplexing may be its peculiar phase, but we shall be able to speak to it and comfort it. He who holds the truth, is usually the most useful man. As a good Presbyterian brother said to me the other day: "I know God has blessed you exceedingly in gathering in souls, but it is an extraordinary fact that nearly all the men I know—with scarcely an exception—who have been made useful in gathering in souls, have held the great doctrines of the grace of God." Almost every man whom God has blessed to the building up of the church in prosperity, and around whom the people have rallied, has been a man who has held firmly free grace from first to last, through the finished salvation of Christ. Do not you think you need have errors in your doctrine to make you useful. We have some who preach Calvinism all the first part of the sermon, and finish up with Arminianism, because they think that will make them useful. Useful nonsense!—That is all it is. A man if he cannot be useful with the truth, cannot be useful with an error. There is enough in the pure doctrine of God, without introducing heresies to preach to sinners. As far as I know, I never felt hampered or cramped in addressing the ungodly in my life. I can speak with as much fervency, and yet not in the same style as those who hold the contrary views of God's truth. Those who hold God's word, never need add something untrue in speaking to men. The sturdy truth of God touches every chord in every man's heart. If we can, by God's grace, put our hand inside man's heart, we want nothing but that whole truth to move him thoroughly, and to stir him up. There is nothing like the real truth and the whole truth, to make a man useful.

II. Now, again, here is a DIFFICULTY SUGGESTED, and

that is—that we require a guide to conduct us into all truth. The difficulty is that truth is not so easy to discover. There is no man born in this world by nature who has the truth in his heart. There is no creature that ever was fashioned, since the fall, who has a knowledge of truth innate and natural. It has been disputed by many philosophers whether there are such things as innate ideas at all. But is of no use disputing as to whether there are any innate ideas of truth. There are none such. There are ideas of everything that is wrong and evil; but in us—that is our flesh—there dwelleth no *good* thing; we are born in sin, and shaped in iniquity, in sin did our mother conceive us. There is nothing in us good, and no tendency to righteousness. Then, since we are not born with the truth, we have the task of searching for it. If we are to be blest by being eminently useful as Christian men, we must be well instructed in matters of revelation; but here is the difficulty—that we cannot follow without a guide the winding paths of truth. Why this?

First, because of *the very great intricacy of truth itself.* Truth itself is no easy thing to discover. Those who fancy they know everything and constantly dogmatise with the spirit of "We are the men, and wisdom will die with us," of course see no difficulties whatever in the system they hold; but I believe, the most earnest student of Scripture will find things in the Bible which puzzle him; however earnestly he reads it, he will see some mysteries too deep for him to understand. He will cry out "Truth! I cannot find thee; I know not where thou art, thou art beyond me; I cannot fully view thee." Truth is a path so narrow that two can scarce walk together in it; we usually tread the narrow way in single file; two men can seldom walk arm in arm in the truth. We believe the same truth in the main but we cannot walk together in the path, it is too narrow. The way of truth is very difficult. If you step an inch aside on the right you are in a dangerous error, and if you swerve a little to the left you are equally in the mire. On the one hand there is a huge precipice, and on the other a deep morass; and unless you keep to the true line, to the breadth of a hair, you will go astray. Truth is a narrow path indeed. It is a path the eagle's eye hath not seen, and a depth the diver hath not visited. It is like the veins of metal in a mine, it is often of excessive thinness, and moreover it runneth not in one continued layer. Lose it once, and you may dig for miles and not discover it again; the eye must watch perpetually the direction of the lode. Grains of truth are like the grains of gold in the rivers of Australia—they must be shaken by the hand of patience, and washed in the stream of honesty, or the fine gold will be mingled with sand. Truth is often mingled with error, and it is hard to distinguish it; but we bless God it is said, "When the Spirit of truth is come, he will guide you into all truth."

Another reason why we need a guide is, <u>*the invidiousness of error*</u>. It easily steals upon us, and, if I may so describe our position, we are often like we were on Thursday night in that tremendous fog. Most of us were feeling for ourselves, and wondering where on earth we were. We could scarcely see an inch before us. We came to a place where there were three turnings. We thought we knew the old spot. There was the lamp-post, and now we must take a sharp turn to the left. But not so. We ought to have gone a little to the right. We have been so often to the same place, that we think we know every flag-stone;—and there's our friend's shop over the way. It is dark, but we think we must be quite right, and all the while we are quite wrong, and find ourselves half-a-mile out of the way. So it is with matters of truth. We think, surely this is the right path; and the voice of the evil one whispers, "that is the way, walk ye in it." You do so, and you find to your great dismay, that instead of the path of truth, you have been walking in the paths of unrighteousness and erroneous doctrines. The way of life is a labyrinth; the grassiest paths and the most bewitching, are the farthest away from right; the most enticing, are those which are garnished with wrested truths. I believe there is not a counterfeit coin in the world so much like a genuine one, as some errors are like the truth. One is base metal, the other is true gold; still in externals they differ very little.

We also need a guide, because *we are so prone to go astray*, Why, if the path of heaven were as straight as Bunyan pictures it, with no turning to the right hand or left—and no doubt it is,—we are so prone to go astray, that we should go to the right hand to the Mountains of Destruction, or to the left in the dark Wood of Desolation. David says, "I have gone astray like a lost sheep." That means very often: for if a sheep is put into a field twenty times, if it does not get out twenty-one times, it will because it cannot; because the place is hurdled up, and it cannot find a hole in the hedge. If grace did not guide a man, he would go astray, though there were hand-posts all the way to heaven. Let it be written, "Miklat, Miklat, the way to refuge," he would turn aside, and the avenger of blood would overtake him, if some guide did not, like the angels in Sodom, put his hand on his shoulders and cry, "Escape, escape, for thy life! look not behind thee; stay not in all the plain." These, then, are the reasons why we need a guide.

III. In the third place, here is A PERSON PROVIDED. This is none other than God, and this God is none other than a person. This person is "he, the Spirit," the "Spirit of truth;" not an influence or an emanation, but actually a person. "When the Spirit of truth is come, he shall guide you into all truth." Now, we wish you to look at this guide, to consider how adapted he is to us.

In the first place, he is *infallible*; he knows everything and cannot lead us astray. If I pin my sleeve to another man's coat, he may lead me part of the way rightly, but by-and-bye he will go wrong himself, and I shall be led astray with him. But if I give myself to the Holy Ghost and ask his guidance, there is no fear of my wandering.

Again, we rejoice in this Spirit because he is *ever-present*.

We fall into a difficulty sometimes; we say, "Oh, if I could take this to my minister, he would explain it; but I live so far off, and am not able to see him." That perplexes us, and we turn the text round and round and cannot make anything out of it. We look at the commentators. We take down pious Thomas Scott, and, as usual, he says nothing about it if it be a dark passage. Then we go to holy Matthew Henry, and if it is an easy Scripture, he is sure to explain it; but if it is a text hard to be understood, it is likely enough, of course, left in his own gloom. And even Dr. Gill himself, the most consistent of commentators, when he comes to a hard passage, manifestly avoids it in some degree. But when we have no commentator or minister, we have still the Holy Spirit. And let me tell you a little secret: whenever you cannot understand a text, open your Bible, bend your knee, and pray over that text; and if it does not split into atoms and open itself, try again. If prayer does not explain it, it is one of the things God did not intend you to know, and you may be content to be ignorant of it. Prayer is the key that openeth the cabinets of mystery. Prayer and faith are sacred picklocks that can open secrets, and obtain great treasures. There is no college for holy education like that of the blessed Spirit, for he is an ever-present tutor, to whom we have only to bend the knee, and he is at our side, the great expositor of truth.

But there is one thing about the suitability of this guide which is remarkable. I do not know whether it has struck you—the Holy Spirit can "guide us *into* a truth." Now, man can guide us *to* a truth, but it is only the Holy Spirit who can "guide us *into* a truth." "When he, the Spirit of truth, shall come, he shall guide you *into*"—mark that word—"all truth." Now, for instance, it is a long while before you can lead some people to election; but when you have made them see its correctness, you have not led them "into" it. You may show them that it is plainly stated in Scripture, but they will turn away and hate it. You take them to another great truth, but they have been brought up in a different fashion, and though they cannot answer your arguments, they say, "The man is right, perhaps," and they whisper—but so low that conscience itself cannot hear—"but it is so contrary to my prejudices, that I cannot receive it." After you have led them *to* the truth, and they see it is true, how hard it is to lead them *into* it! There are many of my hearers who are brought *to* the truth of their depravity; but they are not brought *into* it, and made to feel it. Some of you are brought to know the truth that God keeps us from day to day; but you rarely get into it, so as to live in continual dependence upon God the Holy Ghost, and draw fresh supplies from him. The thing is—to get inside it. A Christian should do with truth as a shall does with his shell—live inside it, as well as carry it on his back, and bear it perpetually about with him. The Holy Ghost, it is said, shall lead us into all truth. You may be brought to a chamber where there is an abundance of gold and silver, but you will be no richer unless you effect an entrance. It is the Spirit's work to unbar the two-leaved gates, and bring us into a truth, so that we may get inside it, and, as dear old Rowland Hill said, "Not only hold the truth, but have the truth hold us."

IV. Fourthly, here is A METHOD SUGGESTED: "He shall guide you into all truth." Now I must have an illustration. I must compare truth to some cave or grotto that you have heard of, with wondrous stalactites hanging from the roof, and others starting from the floor; a cavern, glittering with spar and abounding in marvels. Before entering the cavern you inquire for a guide, who comes with his lighted flambeau. He conducts you down to a considerable depth, and you find yourself in the midst of the cave. He leads you through different chambers. Here he points to a little stream rushing from amid the rocks, and indicates its rise and progress; there he points to some peculiar rock and tells you its name; then takes you into a large natural hall, tells you how many persons once feasted in it; and so on. Truth is a grand series of caverns, it is our glory to have so great and wise a conductor. Imagine that we are coming to the darkness of it. He is a light shining in the midst of us to guide us. And by the light he shows us wondrous things. In three ways the Holy Ghost teaches us: by suggestion, direction, and illumination.

First, he guides us into all truth *by suggesting it*. There are thoughts that dwell in our minds that were not born there, but which were exotics brought from heaven and put there by the spirit. It is not a fancy that angels whisper into our ears, and that devils do the same: both good and evil spirits hold converse with men; and some of us have known it. We have had strange thoughts which were not the off-spring of our souls, but which came from angelic visitants; and direct temptations and evil insinuations have we had which were not brewed in our own souls, but which came from the pestilential cauldron of hell. So the Spirit doth speak in men's ears, sometimes in the darkness of the night. In ages gone by he spoke in dreams and visions, but now he speaketh by his Word. Have you not at times had unaccountably in the middle of your business a thought concerning God and heavenly things, and could not tell whence it came? Have you not been reading or studying the Scripture, but a text came across your mind, and you could not help it; though you even put it down it was like cork in water, and would swim up again to the top of your mind. Well, that good thought was put there by the Spirit; he often guides his people into all truth by suggesting, just as the guide in the grotto does with his flambeau. He does not say a word, perhaps, but he walks into a passage himself, and you follow him; so the Spirit suggests a thought, and your heart follows it up. Well can I remember the manner in which I learned the doctrines of grace in a single instant. Born, as all of us are by nature, an Arminian, I still believed the old things I had heard continually from the pulpit, and did not see the grace of God. I remember sitting one day in the house of God and hearing a sermon as dry as possible, and as worthless as all such sermons are, when a thought struck my mind—how came I to be converted? I prayed, thought I. Then I thought how came I to pray? I was induced to pray by reading the Scriptures. How came I to read the Scriptures? Why—I did read them; and what led me to that? And then, in a moment, I saw that God was at the bottom of all, and that he was the author of faith. And then the whole doctrine opened up to me, from which I have not departed.

But sometimes he leads us *by direction*. The guide points and says—"There, gentlemen, go along that particular path; that is the way." So the Spirit gives a direction and tendency to our thoughts; not suggesting a new one but letting a particular thought when it starts take such-and-such a direction; not so much putting a boat on the stream as steering it when it is there. When our thoughts are considering sacred things he leads us into a more excellent channel from that in which we started. Time after time have you commenced a meditation on a certain doctrine and, unaccountably, you were gradually led away into another, and you saw how one doctrine leaned on another, as is the case with the stones in the arch of a bridge, all hanging on the keystone of Jesus Christ crucified. You were brought to see these things not by a new idea suggested, but by direction given to your thoughts.

But perhaps the best way in which the Holy Ghost leads us into all truth is by *illumination*. He illuminates the Bible. Now, have any of you an illuminated Bible at home? "No," says one, "I have a morocco Bible; I have a Polyglot Bible; I have a marginal reference Bible." Ah! that is all very well; but have you an illuminated Bible? "Yes; I have a large family Bible with pictures in it." There is a picture of John the Baptist baptizing Christ by pouring water on his head and many other nonsensical things; but that is not what I mean: have you an illuminated Bible? "Yes; I have a Bible with splendid engravings in it." Yes; I know you may have; but have you an illuminated Bible? "I don't understand what you mean by an illuminated Bible." Well, it is the Christian man who has an illuminated Bible. He does not buy it illuminated originally, but when he reads it

> "A glory gilds the sacred page,
>   Majestic like the sun;
> Which gives a light to every age,—
>   It gives, but burrows none."

There is nothing like reading an illuminated Bible, beloved. You may read to all eternity, and never learn anything by it, unless it is illuminated by the Spirit; and then the words shine forth like stars. The book seems made of gold leaf; every single letter glitters like a diamond. Oh! it is a blessed thing to read an illuminated Bible lit up by the radiance of the Holy Ghost. Hast thou read the Bible and studied it, my brother, and yet have thine eyes been unenlightened? Go and say, "O Lord, gild the Bible for me. I want an expounded Bible. Illuminate it; shine upon it; for I cannot read it to profit, unless thou enlightenest me." Blind men may read the Bible with their fingers, but blind souls cannot. We want a light to read the Bible by; there is no reading it in the dark. Thus the Holy Spirit leads us into all truth, by suggesting ideas, by directing our thoughts, and by illuminating the Scriptures when we read them.

V. The last thing is AN EVIDENCE. The question arises, How may I know whether I am enlightened by the Spirit's influence, and led into all truth? First, you may know the Spirit's influence by its *unity*—he guides us into all *truth*: secondly, by its *universality*—he guides us into *all* truth.

First, if you are judging a minister, whether he has the Holy Ghost in him or not, you may know him in the first place, by *the constant unity of his testimony.* A man cannot be enlightened by the Holy Spirit, who preaches yea and nay. The Spirit never says one thing at one time and another thing at another time. There are indeed many good men who say both yea and nay; but still their contrary testimonies are not both from God the Spirit, for God the Spirit cannot witness to black and white, to a falsehood and truth. It has been always held as a first principle, that truth is one thing. But some persons say, "I find one thing in one part of the Bible and another thing in another, and though it contradicts itself I must believe it." All quite right, brother, if it did contradict itself; but the fault is not in the wood but in the carpenter. Many carpenters do not understand dove-tailing; so there are many preachers who do not understand dove-tailing. It is very nice work, and it is not easily learnt; it takes some apprenticeship to make all doctrines square together. Some preachers preach very good Calvinism for half-an-hour, and the next quarter-of-an hour Arminianism. If they are Calvinists, let them stick to it; if they are Arminians, let them stick to it; let their preaching be all of a piece. Don't let them pile up things only to kick them all down again; let us have one thing woven from the top throughout, and let us not rend it. How did Solomon know the true mother of the child. "Cut it in halves," said he. The woman who was not the mother, did not care so long as the other did not get the whole, and she consented. "Ah!" said the true mother, "give her the living child. Let her have it, rather than cut it in halves." So the true child of God would say, "I give it up, let my opponent conquer; I do not want to have the truth cut in halves. I would rather be all wrong, than have the word altered to my taste." We do not want to have a divided Bible. No, we claim the whole living child or none at all. We may rest assured of this, that until we get rid of our linsey-wolsey doctrine, and cease to sow mingled seed, we shall not have a blessing. An enlightened mind cannot believe a gospel which denies itself; it must be one thing or the other. One thing cannot contradict another, and yet it and its opposite be equally true. You may know the Spirit's influence, then, by the unity of its testimony.

And you may know it by its *universality*. The true child

of God will not be led into some truth but into all truth. When first he starts he will not know half the truth, he will believe it but not understand it; he will have the germ of it but not the sum total in all its breadth and length. There is nothing like learning by experience. A man cannot set up for a theologian in a week. Certain doctrines take years to develop themselves. Like the aloe that taketh a hundred years to be dressed, there be some truths that must lie long in the heart before they really come out and make themselves appear so that we can speak of them as that we do know, and testify of that which we have seen. The Spirit will gradually lead us into all truth. For instance, if it be true that Jesus Christ is to reign upon the earth personally for a thousand years, as I am inclined to believe it is, if I be under the Spirit, that will be more and more opened to me, until I with confidence declare it. Some men begin very timidly. A man says, at first, "I know we are justified by faith, and have peace with God, but so many have cried out against eternal justification, that I am afraid of it." But he is gradually enlightened, and led to see that in the same hour when all his debts were paid, a full discharge was given; that in the moment when its sin was cancelled, every elect soul was justified in God's mind, though they were not justified in their own minds till afterwards. The Spirit shall lead you into all truth.

Now, what are the practical inferences from this great doctrine? The first is with reference to the Christian who is afraid of his own ignorance. How many are there who are just enlightened and have tasted of heavenly things, who are afraid they are too ignorant to he saved! Beloved, God the Holy Spirit can teach any one, however illiterate, however uninstructed. I have known some men who were almost idiots before conversion, but they afterwards had their faculties wonderfully developed. Some time ago there was a man who was so ignorant that he could not read, and he never spoke anything like grammar in his life, unless by mistake; and moreover, he was considered to be what the people in his neighbourhood called "daft." But when he was converted, the first thing he did was to pray. He stammered out a few words, and in a little time his powers of speaking began to develop themselves. Then he thought he would like to read the Scriptures, and after long, long months of labor, he learned to read. And what was the next thing? He thought he could preach; and he did preach a little in his own homely way, in his house. Then he thought "I must read a few more books." And so his mind expanded, until, I believe he is at the present day, a useful minister, settled in a country village, laboring for God. It needs but little intellect to be taught of God. If you feel your ignorance, do not despair. Go to the Spirit—the great Teacher—and ask his sacred influence; and it shall come to pass that he "shall guide you into all truth."

Another inference is this: whenever any of our brethren do not understand the truth let us take a hint as to the best way of dealing with them. Do not let us controvert with them. I have heard many controversies, but never heard of any good from one of them. We have had controversies with certain men called Secularists, and very strong arguments have been brought against them; but I believe that the day of judgment shall declare that a very small amount of good was ever done by contending with these men. Better let them alone; where no fuel is the fire goeth out; and he that debateth with them puts wood upon the fire. So with regard to Baptism. It is of no avail to quarrel with our Pædo-baptist friends. If we simply pray for them that the God of truth may lead them to see the true doctrine, they will come to it far more easily than by discussions. Few men are taught by controversy, for

> "A man convinced against his will, is of the same
> opinion still."

Pray for them that the Spirit of truth may lead them "into all truth." Do not be angry with your brother, but pray for him; cry, "Lord! open thou his eyes that he may behold wondrous things out of thy law."

Lastly, we speak to some of you who know nothing about the Spirit of truth, nor about the truth itself. It may be that some of you are saying, "We care not much which of you are right, we are happily indifferent to it." Ah! but, poor sinner, if thou knewest the gift of God, and who it was that spake the truth, thou wouldst not say, "I care not for it;" if thou didst know how essential the truth is to thy salvation, thou wouldst not talk so; if thou didst know that the truth of God is—that thou art a worthless sinner, but if thou believest, then God from all eternity, apart from all thy merits, loved thee, and bought thee with the Redeemer's blood, and justified thee in the forum of heaven, and will by-and-bye justify thee in the forum of thy conscience through the Holy Ghost by faith; if thou didst know that there is a heaven for thee beyond the chance of a failure, a crown for thee, the lustre of which can never be dimmed;—then thou wouldst say, "Indeed the truth is precious to my soul!" Why, my ungodly hearers, these men of error want to take away the truth, which alone can save you, the only gospel that can deliver you from hell; they deny the great truths of free-grace, those fundamental doctrines which alone can snatch a sinner from hell; and even though you do not feel interest in them now, I still would say, you ought to desire to see them promoted. May God give you to know the truth in your hearts! May the Spirit "guide you into all truth!" For if you do not know the truth here, recollect there will be a sorrowful learning of it in the dark chambers of the pit, where the only light shall be the flames of hell! May you here know the truth! And the truth shall make you free: and if the Son shall make you free, you shall be free indeed, for he says, "I am the way, the truth, the life." Believe on Jesus thou chief of sinners; trust his love and mercy, and thou art saved, for God the Spirit giveth faith and eternal life.

9
THE HOLY SPIRIT'S CHIEF OFFICE

"He shall glorify me: for he shall receive of mine, and shall shew it unto you. All things that the Father hath are mine: therefore said I, that he shall take of mine, and shall shew it unto you."—John 16:14, 15.

~

IT is the chief office of the Holy Spirit to glorify Christ. He does many things, but this is what he aims at in all of them, to glorify Christ. Brethren, what the Holy Ghost does must be right for us to imitate; therefore, let us endeavour to glorify Christ. To what higher ends can we devote ourselves, than to something to which God the Holy Ghost devotes himself? Be this, then, your continual prayer, "Blessed Spirit, help me ever to glorify the Lord Jesus Christ!"

Observe, that the Holy Ghost glorifies Christ by showing to us the things of Christ. It is a great marvel that there should be any glory given to Christ by showing him to such poor creatures as we are. What! To make us see Christ, does that glorify him? For our weak eyes to behold him, for our trembling hearts to know him, and to love him, does this glorify him? It is even so, for the Holy Ghost chooses this as his principal way of glorifying the

Lord Jesus. He takes of the things of Christ, not to show them to angels, not to write them in letters of fire across the brow of night, but to show them unto us. Within the little temple of a sanctified heart, Christ is praised, not so much by what we do, or think, as by what we see. This puts great value upon meditation, upon the study of God's Word, and upon silent thought under the teaching of the Holy Spirit, for Jesus says, "He shall glorify me: for he shall receive of mine, and shall shew it unto you."

Here is a gospel word at the very outset of our sermon. Poor sinner, conscious of your sin, it is possible for Christ to be glorified by his being shown unto you. If you look to him, if you see him to be a suitable Saviour, an all-sufficient Saviour, if your mind's eye takes him in, if he is effectually shown to you by the Holy Spirit, he is thereby glorified. Sinner as you are, unworthy apparently to become the arena of Christ's glory, yet shall you be a temple in which the King's glory shall be revealed, and your poor heart, like a mirror, shall reflect his grace.

"Come, Holy Spirit, heavenly Dove,
With all thy quickening powers;"

and show Christ to the sinner, that Christ may be glorified in the sinner's salvation!

If that great work of grace is really done at the beginning of the sermon, I shall not mind even if I never finish it. God the Holy Ghost will have wrought more without me than I could possibly have wrought myself, and to the Triune Jehovah shall be all the praise. Oh, that the name of Christ may be glorified in every one of you! Has the Holy Spirit shown you Christ, the Sin-bearer, the one sacrifice for sin, exalted on high, to give repentance and remission? If so, then the Holy Spirit has glorified Christ, even in you.

Now proceeding to examine the text a little in detail, my first observation upon it is this, *the Holy Spirit is our Lord's Glorifier*: "He shall glorify me." Secondly, *Christ's own things are his best glory:* "He shall glorify me: for he shall receive of mine, and shall shew it unto you;" and, thirdly, *Christ's glory is his Father's glory:* "All things that the Father hath are mine: therefore said I, that he shall take of mine, and shall shew it unto you."

I. To begin, then, THE HOLT SPIRIT IS OUR LORD'S GLORIFIER. I want you to keep this truth in your mind, and never to forget it; that which does not glorify Christ is not of the Holy Spirit, and that which is of the Holy Spirit invariably glorifies our Lord Jesus Christ.

First, then, *have an eye to this truth in all comforts.* If a comfort which you think you need, and which appears to you to be very sweet, does not glorify Christ, look very suspiciously upon it. If, in conversing with an apparently religious man, he prates about truth which he says is comforting, but which does not honour Christ, do not you have anything to do with it. It is a poisonous sweet; it may charm you for a moment, but it will ruin your soul for ever if you partake of it. But blessed are those comforts which smell of Christ, those consolations in which there is a fragrance of myrrh, and aloes, and cassia, out of the King's palace, the comfort drawn from his person, from his work, from his blood, from his resurrection, from his glory, the comfort directly fetched from that sacred spot where he trod the winepress alone. This is wine of which you may drink, and forget your misery, and be unhappy no more; but always look with great suspicion upon any comfort offered to you, either as a sinner or a saint, which does not come distinctly from Christ. Say, "I will not be comforted till Jesus comforts me. I will refuse to lay aside my despondency until he removes my sin. I will not go to Mr. Civility, or Mr. Legality, for the unlading of my burden; no hands shall ever lift the load of conscious sin from off my heart but those that were nailed to the cross, when Jesus himself bore my sins in his own body on the tree." Please carry this truth with you wherever you go, as a kind of spiritual litmus paper, by which you may test everything that is presented to you as a cordial or comfort. If it does not glorify Christ, let it not console or please you.

In the next place, *have an eye to this truth in all ministries*. There are many ministries in the world, and they are very diverse from one another; but this truth will enable you to judge which is right out of them all. That ministry which makes much of Christ, is of the Holy Spirit; and that ministry which decries him, ignores him, or puts him in the background in any degree, is not of the Spirit of God. Any doctrine which magnifies man, but not man's Redeemer, any doctrine which denies the depth of the Fall, and consequently derogates from the greatness of salvation, any doctrine which makes sin less, and therefore makes Christ's work less,—away with it, away with it. This shall be your infallible test as to whether it is of the Holy Ghost or not, for Jesus says, "He shall glorify me." It were better to speak five words to the glory of Christ, than to be the greatest orator who ever lived, and to neglect or dishonour the Lord Jesus Christ. We, my brethren, who are preachers of the Word, have but a short time to live; let us dedicate all that time to the glorious work of magnifying Christ. Longfellow says, in his *Psalm of Life*, that "Art is long," but longer still is the great art of lifting up the Crucified before the eyes of the sin-bitten sons of men. Let us keep to that one employment. If we have but this one string upon which we can play, we may discourse such music on it as would ravish angels, and will save men; therefore, again I say, let us keep to that alone. Cornet, flute, harp, sackbut, psaltery, dulcimer, and all kinds of music are for Nebuchadnezzar's golden image; but as for our God, our one harp is Christ Jesus. We will touch every string of that wondrous instrument, even though it be with trembling fingers, and marvellous shall be the music we shall evoke from it.

All ministries, therefore, must be subjected to this test; if they do not glorify Christ, they are not of the Holy Ghost.

We should also *have an eye to this truth in all religious movements*, and judge them by this standard. If they are of the Holy Spirit, they glorify Christ. There are great movements in the world every now and then; we are inclined to look upon them hopefully, for any stir is better than stagnation; but, by-and-by we begin to fear, with a holy jealousy, what their effects will be. How shall we judge them? To what test shall we put them? Always to this test. Does this movement glorify Christ? Is Christ preached? Then therein I do rejoice, yea, and will rejoice. Are men pointed to Christ? Then this is the ministry of salvation. Is he preached as first and last? Are men bidden to be justified by faith in him, and then to follow him, and copy his divine example? It is well. I do not believe that any man ever lifted up the cross of Christ in a hurtful way. If it be but the cross that is seen, it is the sight of the cross, not of the hands that lift it, that will bring salvation. Some modern movements are heralded with great noise, and some come quietly; but if they glorify Christ, it is well. But, dear friends, if it is some new theory that is propounded, if it is some old error revived, if it is something very glittering and fascinating, and for a while it bears the multitudes away, think nothing of it; unless it glorifies Christ it is not for you and me. "*Aliquid Christi*," as one of the old fathers said, "Anything of Christ," and I love it; but nothing of Christ, or something against Christ, then it may be very fine and flowery, and it may be very fascinating and charming, highly poetical, and in consonance with the spirit of the age; but we say of it, "Vanity of vanities, all is vanity where there is no Christ." Where he is uplifted, there is all that is wanted for the salvation of a guilty race. Judge every movement, then, not by those who adhere to it, nor by those who admire and praise it, but by this word of our Lord, "He shall glorify me." The Spirit of God is not in it if it does not glorify Christ.

Once again, brethren, I pray you, *eye this truth when you are under a sense of great weakness*, physical, mental, or spiritual. You have finished preaching a sermon, you have completed a round with your tracts, or you have ended your Sunday-school work for another Sabbath. You say to yourself, "I fear that I have done very poorly." You groan as you go to your bed because you think that you have not glorified Christ. It is as well that you should groan if that is the case. I will not forbid it, but I will relieve the bitterness of your distress by reminding you that it is the Holy Ghost who is to glorify Christ: "He shall glorify me." If I preach, and the Holy Spirit is with me, Christ will be glorified; but if I were able to speak with the tongues of men, and of angels, but without the power of the Holy Ghost, Christ would not be glorified. Sometimes, our weakness may even help to make way for the greater display of the might of God. If so, we may glory in infirmity, that the power of Christ may rest upon us. It is not merely we who speak, but the Spirit of the Lord, who speaketh by us. There is a sound of abundance of rain outside the Tabernacle; would God that there were also the sound of abundance of rain within our hearts! May the Holy Spirit come at this moment, and come at all times whenever his servants are trying to glorify Christ, and himself do what must always be his own work! How can you and I glorify anybody, much less glorify him who is infinitely glorious? But the Holy Ghost, being himself the glorious God, can glorify the glorious Christ. It is a work worthy of God; and it shows us, when we think of it, the absolute need of our crying to the Holy Spirit that he would take us in his hand, and use us as a workman uses his hammer. What can a hammer do without the hand that grasps it, and what can we do without the Spirit of God?

I will make only one more observation upon this first point. If the Holy Spirit is to glorify Christ, I beg you to *have an eye to this truth amid all oppositions, controversies, and contentions.* If we alone had the task of glorifying Christ, we might be beaten; but as the Holy Spirit is the Glorifier of Christ, his glory is in very safe hands. "Why do the heathen rage, and the people imagine a vain thing?" The Holy Spirit is still to the front; the eternal purpose of God to set his King upon the throne, and to make Jesus Christ reign for ever and ever, must be fulfilled, for the Holy Ghost has undertaken to see it accomplished. Amidst the surging tumults of the battle, the result of the conflict is never in doubt for a moment. It may seem as though the fate of Christ's cause hung in a balance, and that the scales were in equilibrium; but it is not so. The glory of Christ never wanes; it must increase from day to day, as it is made known in the hearts of men by the Holy Spirit; and the day shall come when Christ's praise shall go up from all human tongues. To him every knee shall bow, and every tongue shall confess that Jesus Christ is Lord, to the glory of God the Father. Therefore, lift up the hands that hang down, and confirm the feeble knees. If *you* have failed to glorify Christ by your speech as you would, there is Another who has done it, and who will still do it, according to Christ's words, "He shall glorify me." My text seems to be a silver bell, ringing sweet comfort into the dispirited worker's ear, "He shall glorify me."

That is the first point, the Holy Spirit is our Lord's Glorifier. Keep that truth before your mind's eye under all circumstances.

II. Now, secondly, CHRIST'S OWN THINGS ARE HIS BEST GLORY. When the Holy Spirit wants to glorify Christ, what does he do? He does not go abroad for anything, he comes to Christ himself for that which will be for Christ's own glory: "He shall glorify me: for he shall receive of mine, and shall shew it unto you." There can be no glory added to Christ; it must be his own glory, which he has already, which is made more apparent to the hearts of God's chosen by the Holy Spirit.

First of all, *Christ needs no new inventions to glorify him.* "We have struck out a new line of things," says one. Have you? "We have found out something very wonderful." I dare say you have; but Christ, the same yesterday, to-day, and for ever, wants none of your inventions, or discoveries, or additions to his truth. A plain Christ is ever the loveliest Christ. Dress him up, and you have deformed him and defamed him. Bring him out just as he is, the Christ of God, nothing else but Christ, unless you bring in his cross, for we preach Christ crucified; indeed, you cannot have the Christ without the cross; but preach Christ crucified, and you have given him all the glory that he wants. The Holy Ghost does not reveal in these last times any fresh ordinances, or any novel doctrines, or any new evolutions; but he simply brings to mind the things which Christ himself spoke, he brings Christ's own things to us, and in that way glorifies him.

Think for a minute of *Christ's person* as revealed to us by the Holy Spirit. What can more glorify him than for us to see his person, very God of very God, and yet as truly man? What a wondrous being, as human as ourselves, but as divine as God! Was there ever another like to him? Never.

Think of his *incarnation*, his birth at Bethlehem. There was greater glory among the oxen in the stall than ever was seen where those born in marble halls were swathed in purple and fine linen. Was there ever another babe like Christ? Never. I wonder not that the wise men fell down to worship him.

Look at his *life*, the standing wonder of all ages. Men, who have not worshipped him, have admired him. His life is incomparable, unique; there is nothing like it in all the history of mankind. Imagination has never been able to invent anything approximating to the perfect beauty of the life of Jesus Christ.

Think of his *death*. There have been many heroic and martyr deaths; but there is not one that can be set side by side with Christ's death. He did not pay the debt of nature as others do; and yet he paid our nature's debt. He did not die because he must; he died because he would. The only "must" that came upon him was a necessity of all-conquering love. The cross of Christ is the greatest wonder of fact or of fiction; fiction invents many marvellous things, but nothing than can be looked at for a moment in comparison with the cross of Christ.

Think of our Lord's *resurrection*. If this be one of the things that are taken, and shown to you by the Holy Spirit, it will fill you with holy delight. I am sure that I could go into that sepulchre, where John and Peter went, and spend a lifetime in reverencing him who broke down the barriers of the tomb, and made it a passage-way to heaven. Instead of being a dungeon and a *cul-de-sac*, into which all men seemed to go, but none could ever come out, Christ has, by his resurrection, made a tunnel right through the grave. Jesus, by dying, has killed death for all believers.

Then think of his *ascension*. But why need I take you over all these scenes with which you are blessedly familiar? What a wondrous fact that, when the cloud received him out of the disciples'sight, the angels came to convoy him to his heavenly home!

> "They brought his chariot from above,
>   To bear him to his throne;
> Clapp'd their triumphant wings, and cried,
>   'The glorious work is done.'"

Think of him now, *at his Father's right hand*, adored of all the heavenly host; and then let your mind fly forward to the glory of his Second Advent, the final judgment with its terrible terrors, the millennium with its indescribable bliss, and the heaven of heavens, with its endless and unparalleled splendour. If these things are shown to you by the Holy Spirit, the beatific visions will indeed glorify Christ, and you will sit down, and sing with the blessed Virgin, "My soul doth magnify the Lord, and my spirit hath rejoiced in God my Saviour."

Thus, you see that the things which glorify Christ are all in Christ; the Holy Spirit fetches nothing from abroad, but he takes of the things of Christ, and shows them unto us. The glory of kings lies in their silver and their gold, their silk and their gems; but the glory of Christ lies in himself. If we want to glorify a man, we bring him presents; if we wish to glorify Christ, we must accept presents from him. Thus we take the cup of salvation, calling upon the name of the Lord, and in so doing we glorify Christ.

Notice, next, that *these things of Christ's are too bright for us to see till the Spirit shows them to us*. We cannot see them because of their excessive glory, until the Holy Spirit tenderly reveals them to us, until he takes of the things of Christ, and shows them to us.

What does this mean? Does it not mean, first, that he enlightens our understandings? It is wonderful how the Holy Spirit can take a fool, and make him know the wonders of Christ's dying love; and he does make him know it very quickly when he begins to teach him. Some of us have been very slow learners, yet the Holy Spirit has been able to teach something even to us. He opens the Scriptures, and he also opens our minds; and when there are these two openings together, what a wonderful opening it is! It becomes like a new revelation; the first is the revelation of the letter, which we have in the Book; the second is the revelation of the Spirit, which we get in our own spirit. O my dear friend, if the Holy Ghost has ever enlightened your understanding, you know what it is for him to show the things of Christ to you!

But next, he does this by a work upon the whole soul. I mean this. When the Holy Ghost convinces us of sin, we become fitted to see Christ, and so the blessed Spirit shows Christ to us. When we are conscious of our feebleness, then we see Christ's strength; and thus the Holy Ghost shows him to us. Often, the operations of the Spirit of God may seem not to be directly the showing of Christ to us, but as they prepare us for seeing him, they are a part of the work.

The Holy Ghost sometimes shows Christ to us by his

power of vivifying the truth. I do not know whether I can quite tell you what I mean; but I have sometimes seen a truth differently from what I have ever seen it before. I knew it long ago, I owned it as part of the divine revelation; but now I realize it, grip it, grasp it, or what is better, it seems to get a grip of me, and hold me in its mighty hands. Have you not sometimes been overjoyed with a promise which never seemed anything to you before? Or a doctrine, which you believed, but never fully appreciated, has suddenly become to you a gem of the first water, a very Koh-i-Noor, or, "Mountain of Light." The Holy Spirit has a way of focussing light, and when it falls in this special way upon a certain point, then the truth is revealed to us. He shall take of the things of Christ, and show them unto you. Have you never felt ready to jump for joy, ready to start from your seat, ready to sit up in your bed at night, and sing praises to God through the overpowering influence of some grand old truth which has seemed to be all at once quite new to you?

The Holy Spirit also shows to us the things of Christ in our experience. As we journey on in life, we pass up hill and down dale, through bright sunlight and through dark shadows, and in each of these conditions we learn a little more of Christ, a little more of his grace, a little more of his glory, a little more of his sin-bearing, a little more of his glorious righteousness. Blessed is the life which is just one long lesson upon the glory of Christ; and I think that is what every Christian life should be. "Every dark and bending line" in our experience should meet in the centre of Christ's glory, and should lead us nearer and nearer to the power of enjoying the bliss at his right hand for ever and ever. Thus the Holy Spirit takes of the things of Christ, and shows them to us, and so glorifies Christ.

Beloved, the practical lesson for us to learn is this, *let us try to abide under the influence of the Holy Spirit.* To that end, let us think very reverently of him. Some never think of him at all. How many sermons there are without even an allusion to him! Shame on the preachers of such discourses! If any hearers come without praying for the Holy Spirit, shame on such hearers! We know and we confess that he is everything to our spiritual life; then why do we not remember him with greater love, and worship him with greater honour, and think of him continually with greater reverence? Beware of committing the sin against the Holy Ghost. If any of you feel any gentle touches of his power when you are hearing a sermon, beware lest you harden your heart against it. Whenever the sacred fire comes as but a spark, quench not the Holy Spirit, but pray that the spark may become a flame. And you, Christian people, do cry to him that you may not read your Bibles without his light. Do not pray without being helped by the Spirit; above all, may you never preach without the Holy Spirit! It seems a pity when a man asks to be guided of the Spirit in his preaching, and then pulls out a manuscript, and reads it. The Holy Spirit may bless what he reads; but he cannot very well guide him when he has tied himself down to what he has written. And it will be the same with the speaker if he only repeats what he has learnt, and leaves no room for the Spirit to give him a new thought, a fresh revelation of Christ; how can he hope for the divine blessing under such circumstances? Oh, it were better for us to sit still until some of us were moved by the Spirit to get up and speak, than for us to prescribe the methods by which he should speak to us, and even to write down the very words we mean to utter! What room is there for the Spirit's operations then?

"Come, Holy Spirit, heavenly Dove,"

I cannot help breaking out into that prayer, "Blessed Spirit, abide with us, take of the things of Christ, and show them to us, that so Christ may be glorified."

III. I am only going to speak a minute or two on the last point. It is a very deep one, much too deep for me. I am unable to take you into the depths of my text, I will not pretend to do so; I believe that there are meanings here which probably we shall never understand till we get to heaven. "What thou knowest not now, thou shalt know hereafter." But this is the point, CHRIST'S GLORY IS HIS FATHER'S GLORY: "All things that the Father hath are mine: therefore said I, that he shall take of mine, and shall shew it unto you."

First, *Christ has all that the Father has.* Do think of that. No mere man dares to say, "All things that the Father hath are mine." All the Godhead is in Christ; not only all the attributes of it, but the essence of it. The Nicene Creed well puts it, and it is not too strong in the expression: "Light of Light, very God of very God," for Christ has all that the Father has. When we come to Christ, we come to omnipotent omnipresent omniscience; we come to almighty immutability; we come, in fact, to the eternal Godhead. The Father has all things, and all power is given unto Christ in heaven and on earth, so that he has all that the Father has.

And, further, *the Father is glorified in Christ's glory.* Never let us fall into the false notion that, if we magnify Christ, we are depreciating the Father. If any lips have ever spoken concerning the Christ of God so as to depreciate the God of Christ, let those lips be covered with shame. We never did preach Christ up as merciful, and the Father as only just, or Christ as moving the Father to be gracious. That is a slander which has been cast upon us, but there is not an atom of truth in it. We have known and believed what Christ himself said, "I and my Father are one." The more glorious Christ is, the more glorious the Father is; and when men, professedly Christians, begin to cast off Christ, they cast off God the Father to a large extent. Irreverence to the Son of God soon becomes irreverence to God the Father himself. But, dear friends, we delight to honour Christ, and we will continue to do so. Even when we stand in the heaven of heavens, before the burning throne of the infinite Jehovah, we will sing praises unto him and unto the Lamb, putting the two evermore in that divine conjunction in which they are always to be found.

Thus, you see, Christ has all that the Father has, and when he is glorified, the Father also is glorified.

Next, *the Holy Spirit must lead us to see this*, and I am sure that he will. If we give ourselves up to his teaching, we shall fall into no errors. It will be a great mystery, but we shall know enough, so that it will never trouble us. If you sit down and try to study the mystery of the Eternal, well, I believe that the longer you look, the more you will be like persons who look into the sea from a great height, until they grow dizzy, and are ready to fall and to be drowned. Believe what the Spirit teaches you, and adore your Divine Teacher; then shall his instruction become easy to you. I believe that, as we grow older, we come to worship God as Abraham did, as Jehovah, the great I AM. Jesus does not fade into the background; but the glorious Godhead seems to become more and more apparent to us. Our Lord's word to his disciples, "Ye believe in me, believe also in God." And as we come to a full confidence in the glorious Lord, the God of nature, and of providence, and of redemption, and of heaven, the Holy Spirit gives us to know more of the glories of Christ.

I have talked with you as well as I could upon this sublime theme, and if I did not know that the Holy Spirit glorifies Christ, I should go home miserable, for I have not been able to glorify my Lord as I would; but I know that the Holy Spirit can take what I have said out of my very heart, and can put it into your hearts, and he can add to it whatever I have omitted. Go ye who love the Lord, and glorify him. Try to do it by your lips and by your lives. Go ye, and preach him, preach more of him, and preach him up higher, and higher, and higher. The old lady, of whom I have heard, made a mistake in what she said, yet there was a truth behind her blunder. She had been to a little Baptist chapel, where a high Calvinist preached, and on coming away she said that she liked "High Calvary" preachers best.

So do I. Give me a "High Calvary" preacher, one who will make Calvary the highest of all the mountains. I suppose it was not a hill at all, but only a mound; still, let us lift it higher and higher, and say to all other hills, "Why leap ye, ye high hills? This is the hill which God desires to dwell in; yea, the Lord will dwell in it for ever." The crucified Christ is wiser than all the wisdom of the world. The cross of Christ has more novelty in it than all the fresh things of the earth. O believers and preachers of the gospel, glorify Christ! May the Holy Ghost help you to do so!

And you, poor sinners, who think that you cannot glorify Christ at all, come and trust him,—

"Come naked, come filthy, come just as you are,"

and believe that he will receive you; for that will glorify him. Believe, even now, O sinner at death's door, that Christ can make thee live; for thy faith will glorify him! Look up out of the awful depths of hell into which conscience has cast thee, and believe that he can pluck thee out of the horrible pit, and out of the miry clay, and set thy feet upon a rock; for thy trust will glorify him! It is in the power of the sinner to give Christ the greatest glory, if the Holy Spirit enables him to believe in the Lord Jesus Christ. Thou mayest come, thou who art more leprous, more diseased, more corrupt, than any other; and if thou lookest to him, and he saves thee, oh, then thou wilt praise him! You will be of the mind of the one I have spoken of many times, who said to me, "Sir, you say that Christ can save me. Well, if he does, he shall never hear the last of it." No, and he never will hear the last of it. Blessed Jesus,—

"I will love thee in life, I will love thee in death,
And praise thee as long as thou lendest me breath;
And say when the death-dew lies cold on my brow,
If ever I loved thee, my Jesus, 'tis now."

"In mansions of glory and endless delight,

I'll ever adore thee in heaven so bright;
I'll sing with the glittering crown on my brow,
If ever I loved thee, my Jesus, 'tis now."

We will do nothing else but praise Christ, and glorify him, if he will but save us from sin. God grant that it may be so with every one of us, for the Lord Jesus Christ's sake! Amen.

10
THE NECESSITY OF THE SPIRIT'S WORK

"And I will put my Spirit within you."—*Ezekiel 36:27.*

~

THE miracles of Christ are remarkable for one fact, namely, that they are none of them unnecessary. The pretended miracles of Mahomet, and of the church of Rome, even if they had been miracles, would have been pieces of folly. Suppose that Saint Denis had walked with his head in his hand after it had been cut off, what practical purpose would have been subserved thereby? He would certainly have been quite as well in his grave, for any practical good he would have conferred on men. The miracles of Christ were never unnecessary. They are not freaks of power; they are displays of power it is true, but they all of them have a practical end. The same thing may be said of the promises of God. We have not one promise in the Scripture which may be regarded as a mere freak of grace. As every miracle was necessary, absolutely necessary, so is every promise that is given in the Word of God. And hence from the text that is before us, may I draw, and I think very conclusively, the argument, that if

God in his covenant made with his people has promised to put his Spirit within them, it must be absolutely necessary that this promise should have been made, and it must be absolutely necessary also to our salvation that every one of us should receive the Spirit of God. This shall be the subject of this morning's discourse. I shall not hope to make it very interesting, except to those who are anxiously longing to know the way of salvation.

We start, then, by laying down this proposition—that the work of the Holy Spirit is absolutely necessary to us, if we would be saved.

1. In endeavouring to prove this, I would first of all make the remark that this is very manifest if we *remember what man is by nature*. Some say that man may of himself attain unto salvation—that if he hear the Word, it is in his power to receive it, to believe it, and to have a saving change worked in him by it. To this we reply, you do not know what man is by nature, otherwise you would never have ventured upon such an assertion. Holy Scripture tells us that man by nature is *dead* in trespasses and sins. It does not say that he is sick, that he is faint, that he has grown callous, and hardened, and seared, but it says he is absolutely dead. Whatever that term "death "means in connexion with the body, that it means in connection with man's soul, viewing it in its relation to spiritual things. When the body is dead it is powerless; it is unable to do anything for itself; and when the soul of man is dead, in a spiritual sense, it must be, if there is any meaning in the figure, utterly and entirely powerless, and unable to do anything of itself or for itself. When ye shall see dead men raising themselves from their graves, when ye shall see them unwinding their own sheets, opening their own coffin lids, and walking down our streets alive and animate, as the result of their own power, then perhaps ye may believe that souls that are dead in sin may turn to God, may recreate their own natures, and may make themselves heirs of heaven, though before they were heirs of wrath.

But mark, *not till then*. The drift of the gospel is, that man is dead in sin, and that divine life is God's gift; and you must go contrary to the whole of that drift, before you can suppose a man brought to know and love Christ, apart from the work of the Holy Spirit. The Spirit finds men as destitute of spiritual life as Ezekiel's dry bones; he brings bone to bone, and fits the skeleton together, and then he comes from the four winds and breathes into the slain, and they live, and stand upon their feet, an exceeding great army, and worship God. But apart from that, apart from the vivifying influence of the Spirit of God, men's souls must lie in the valley of dry bones, dead, and dead for ever.

But Scripture does not only tell us that man is dead in sin; it tells us something worse than this, namely, that he is utterly and entirely averse to everything that is good and right. "The carnal mind is enmity against God; for it is not subject to the law of God, neither indeed can be."—Romans 8:7. Turn you all Scripture through, and you find continually the will of man described as being contrary to the things of God. What said Christ in that text so often quoted by the Arminian to disprove the very doctrine which it clearly states? What did Christ say to those who imagined that men would come without divine influence? He said, first, "No man can come unto me except the Father which hath sent me draw him;" but he said something more strong—"Ye *will not* come unto me that ye might have life." No man *will* come. Here lies the deadly mischief; not only that he is powerless to do good, but that he is powerful enough to do that which is wrong, and that his will is desperately set against everything that is right. Go, Arminian, and tell your hearers that they will come if they please, but know that your Redeemer looks you in the face, and tells you that you are uttering a lie. Men will *not* come. They never will come of themselves. You cannot induce them to come; you cannot force them to come by all your thunders, nor can you entice them to come by all your invitations. They *will not* come unto Christ, that they may have life. Until the Spirit draw them, come they neither will, nor can.

Hence, then, from the fact that man's nature is hostile to the divine Spirit, that he hates grace, that he despises the way in which grace is brought to him, that it is contrary to his own proud nature to stoop to receive salvation by the deeds of another—hence it is necessary that the Spirit of God should operate to change the will, to correct the bias of the heart, to set man in a right track, and then give him strength to run in it. Oh! if ye read man and understand him, ye cannot help being sound on the point of the necessity of the Holy Spirit's work. It has been well remarked by a great writer, that he never knew a man who held any great theological error, who did not also hold a doctrine which diminished the depravity of man. The Arminian says man is fallen, it is true, but then he has power of will left, and that will is free; he can raise himself. He diminishes the desperate character of the fall of man. On the other hand, the Antinomian says, man cannot do anything, but that he is not at all responsible, and is not bound to do it, it is not his duty to believe, it is not his duty to repent. Thus, you see, he also diminishes the sinfulness of man; and has not right views of the fall. But once get the correct view, that man is utterly fallen, powerless, guilty, defiled, lost, condemned, and you *must* be sound on all points of the great gospel of Jesus Christ. Once believe man to be what the Scripture says he is—once believe his heart to be depraved, his affections perverted, his understanding darkened, his will perverse, and *you must* hold that if such a wretch as that be saved, it must be the work of the Spirit of God, and of the Spirit of God alone.

2. I have another proof ready to hand. Salvation must be the work of the Spirit in us, because *the means used in salvation are of themselves inadequate for the acccomplishment of the work.* And what are the means of salvation? Why, first and foremost stands the preaching of the Word of God. More

men are brought to Christ by preaching than by anything else; for it is God's chief and first instrument. This is the sword of the Spirit, quick and powerful, to the dividing asunder of the joints and marrow. "It pleaseth God by the foolishness of preaching to save them that believe." But what is there in preaching, by which souls are saved, that looks as if it would be the means of saving souls? I could point you to divers churches and chapels into which you might step, and say "Here is a learned minister indeed, a man who would instruct and enlighten the intellect," you sit down, and you say, "Well, if God means to work a great work he will use a learned man like this." But do you know any learned men that are made the means of bringing souls to Christ, to any great degree? Go round your churches, if you please, and look at them, and then answer the question. Do you know any great men—men great in learning and wisdom—who have become spiritual fathers in our Israel? Is it not a fact that stares us in the face, that our fashionable preachers, our eloquent preachers, our learned preachers, are just the most useless men in creation for the winning of souls to Christ. And where are souls born to God? Why, in the house around which the jeer and the scoff and the sneer of the world have long gathered. Sinners are converted under the man whose eloquence is rough and homely, and who has nothing to commend him to his fellows, who has daily to fall on his knees and confess his own folly, and when the world speaks worst of him, feels that he deserves it all, since he is nothing but an earthen vessel, in which God is pleased to put his heavenly treasure. I will dare to say it, that in every age of the world the most despised ministry has been the most useful; and I could find you at this day poor Primitive Methodist preachers who can scarce speak correct English, who have been the fathers of more souls, and have brought to Christ more than any one bishop on the bench. Why, the Lord hath been pleased always to make it so, that he will clothe with power the weak and the foolish, but he will not clothe with power those who, if good were done, might be led to ascribe the excellence of the power to their learning, their eloquence, or their position. Like the apostle Paul, it is every minister's business to glory in his infirmities. The world says, "Pshaw! upon your oratory, it is rough, and rude, and eccentric." Yes, 'tis even so, but we are content, for God blesses it. Then so much the better that it has infirmities in it; for now shall it be plainly seen that it is not of man or by man, but the work of God, and of God alone. It is said that once upon a time a man exceedingly curious desired to see the sword with which a mighty hero had fought some desperate battles; casting his eye along the blade, he said, "Well, I don't see much in this sword." "Nay," said the hero, "but you have not examined the arm that wields it." And so when men come to hear a successful minister, they are apt to say, "I do not see anything in him." No, but you have not examined the eternal arm that reaps its harvest with this sword of the Spirit. If ye had looked at the jaw-bone of the ass in Samson's hand, you would have said, "What! heaps on heaps with this?" No; bring out some polished blade; bring forth the Damascus steel! No; but God would have all the glory, and, therefore, not with the polished steel, but with the jaw-bone must Samson get the victory. So with ministers; God has usually blessed the weakest to do the most good. Well, now, does it not follow from this, that it must be the work of the Spirit? Because, if there be nothing in the instrument that can lead thereunto, is it not the work of the Spirit when the thing is accomplished? Let me just put it to you. Under the ministry dead souls are quickened, sinners are made to repent, the vilest of sinners are made holy, men who came determined not to believe are compelled to believe. Now, who does this? If you say the ministry does it, then I say farewell to your reason, because there is nothing in the successful ministry which would tend thereunto. It must be that the Spirit worketh in man through the ministry, or else such deeds would never be accomplished. You might as well expect to raise the dead by whispering in their ears, as hope to save souls by preaching to them, if it were not for the agency of the Spirit. Melancthon went out to preach, you know, without the Spirit of the Lord, and he thought he should convert all the people; but he found out at last that old Adam was too strong for young Melancthon, and he had to go back and ask for the help of the Holy Spirit or ever he saw a soul saved. I say, that the fact that the ministry is blessed, proves, since there is nothing in the ministry, that salvation must be the work of a higher power.

Other means, however, are made use of to bless men's souls. For instance, the two ordinances of Baptism and the Lord's Supper. They are both made a rich means of grace. But let me ask you, is there anything in baptism that can possibly bless anybody? Can immersion in water have the slightest tendency to be blessed to the soul? And then with regard to the eating of bread and the drinking of wine at the Lord's Supper, can it by any means be conceived by any rational man that there is anything in the mere piece of bread that we eat, or in the wine that we drink? And yet doubtless the grace of God does go with both ordinances for the confirming of the faith of those who receive them, and even for the conversion of those who look upon the ceremony. There must be something, then, beyond the outward ceremony, there must, in fact, be the Spirit of God, witnessing through the water, witnessing through the wine, witnessing through the bread, or otherwise none of these things could be means of grace to our souls. They could not edify; they could not help us to commune with Christ; they could not tend to the conviction of sinners, or to the establishment of saints. There must then, from these facts, be a higher, unseen, mysterious influence—the influence of the divine Spirit of God.

3. Let me again remind you, in the third place, that the absolute necessity of the work of the Holy Spirit in the

heart may be clearly seen from this fact, that *all which has been done by God the Father, and all that has been done by God the Son must be ineffectual to us, unless the Spirit shall reveal these things to our souls.* We believe, in the first place, that God the Father elects his people; from before all worlds he chooses them to himself; but let me ask you—what effect does the doctrine of election have upon any man, until the Spirit of God enters into him? How do I know whether God has chosen me from before the foundation of the world? How can I possibly know? Can I climb to heaven, and read the roll? Is it possible for me to force my way through the thick mists which hide eternity, and open the seven seals of the book, and read my name recorded there? Ah! no; election is a dead letter both in my consciousness and in any effect which it can produce upon me, until the Spirit of God calls me out of darkness into marvellous light. And then through my calling, I see my election, and knowing myself to be called of God, I know myself to have been chosen of God from before the foundation of the world. It is a precious thing—that doctrine of election—to a child of God. But what makes it precious? Nothing but the influence of the Spirit. Until the Spirit opens the eye to read, until the Spirit imparts the mystic secret, no heart can know its election. No angel ever revealed to any man that he was chosen of God; but the Spirit doth it. He, by his divine workings, bears an infallible witness with our spirits that we are born of God; and then we are enabled to "read our title clear to mansions in the skies."

Look, again, at the covenant of grace. We know that there was a covenant made with the Lord Jesus Christ, by his Father, from before all worlds, and that in this covenant the persons of all his people were given to him, and were secured; but of what use, or of what avail is the covenant to us, until the Holy Spirit brings the blessings of the covenant to us? The covenant is, as it were, a lofty tree laden with fruit; if the Spirit doth not shake that tree and make the fruit fall therefrom until it comes to the level of our standing, how can we receive it? Bring hither any sinner and tell him there is a covenant of grace, what is he advantaged thereby? "Ah," says he, "I may not be included in it; my name may not be recorded there; I may not be chosen in Christ;" but let the Spirit of God dwell in his heart, richly by faith and love which is in Christ Jesus, and that man sees the covenant, ordered in all things and sure, and he cries with David, "It is all my salvation and all my desire."

Take, again, the redemption of Christ. We know that Christ did stand in the room, place, and stead of all his people, and that all those who shall appear in heaven, will appear there as an act of justice as well as of grace, seeing that Christ was punished in their room and stead, and that it would have been unjust if God punished them, seeing that he had punished Christ for them. We believe that Christ having paid all their debts, they have a right to their freedom in Christ—that Christ having covered them with his righteousness, they are entitled to eternal life as much as if they had themselves been perfectly holy. But of what avail is this to me, until the Spirit takes of the things of Christ and shows them to me? What is Christ's blood to any of you, until you have received the Spirit of grace? You have heard the minister preach about the blood of Christ a thousand times, but you passed by; it was nothing to you that Jesus should die. You know that he did atone for sins that were not his own; but you only regarded it as a tale, perhaps, even an idle tale. But when the Spirit of God led you to the cross, and opened your eyes, and enabled you to see Christ crucified, ah, then there was something in the blood indeed. When his hand dipped the hyssop in the blood, and when it applied that blood to your spirit, then there was a joy and peace in believing, such as you had never known before. But ah, my hearer, Christ's dying is nothing to thee, unless thou hast a living Spirit within thee. Christ brings thee no advantage, saving, personal, and lasting, unless the Spirit of God hath baptized thee in the fountain filled with his blood, and washed thee from head to foot therein.

I only mention these few out of the many blessings of the covenant, just to prove that they are none of them of any use to us, unless the Holy Spirit gives them to us. There hang the blessings on the nail—on the nail Christ Jesus; but we are short of stature; we cannot reach them; the Spirit of God takes them down and gives them to us, and there they are; they are ours. It is like the manna in the skies, far out of mortal reach; but the Spirit of God opens the windows of heaven, brings down the bread, and puts it to our lips, and enables us to eat. Christ's blood and righteousness are like wine stored in the wine-vat; but we cannot get thereat. The Holy Spirit dips our vessel into this precious wine, and then we drink; but without the Spirit we must die and perish just as much, though the Father elect and the Son redeem, as though the Father never had elected, and though the Son had never bought us with his blood. The Spirit is absolutely necessary. Without him neither the works of the Father, nor of the Son. are of any avail to us.

4. This brings us to another point. *The experience of the true Christian is a reality; but it never can be known and felt without the Spirit of God.* For what is the experience of the Christian? Let me just give a brief picture of some of its scenes. There is a person come into this hall this morning—one of the most reputable men in London. He has never committed himself in any outward vice; he has never been dishonest; but he is known as a staunch upright tradesman. Now, to his astonishment, he is informed that he is a condemned, lost sinner, and just as surely lost as the thief who died for his crimes upon the cross. Do you think that man will believe it? Suppose, however, that he does believe it, simply because he reads it in the Bible, do you think that man will ever be made to feel it? I know you say, "Impossible!" Some of you, even now, perhaps, are saying, "Well, I never should!" Can you imagine that honourable,

upright tradesman, saying, "God be merciful to me, a sinner?"—standing side-by-side with the harlot and the swearer, and feeling in his own heart as if he had been as guilty as they were, and using just the same prayer, and saying, "Lord, save, or I perish." You cannot conceive it, can you? It is contrary to nature that a man who has been so good as he should put himself down among the chief of sinners. Ah! but that will be done before he will be saved; he must feel that before he can enter heaven. Now, I ask, who can bring him to such a levelling experience as that, but the Spirit of God? I know very well, proud nature will not stoop to it. We are all aristocrats in our own righteousness; we do not like to bend down and come among common sinners. If we are brought there, it must be the Spirit of God who casts us to the ground. Why, I know if any one had told me that I should ever cry to God for mercy, and confess that I had been the vilest of the vile, I should have laughed in their face; I should have said, "Why, I have not done anything particularly wrong; I have not hurt anybody." And yet I know this very day I can take my place upon the lowest form, and if I can get inside heaven I shall feel happy to sit among the chief of sinners, and praise that Almighty love which has saved even me from my sins. Now, what works this humiliation of heart? Grace. It is contrary to nature for an honest and an upright man in the eye of the world to feel himself a lost sinner. It must be the Holy Spirit's work, or else it never will be done. Well, after a man has been brought here, can you conceive that man at last conscience-stricken, and led to believe that his past life deserves the wrath of God? His first thought would be, "Well, now, I will live better than I ever have lived." He would say, "Now, I will try and play the hermit, and pinch myself here and there, and deny myself, and do penance; and in that way, by paying attention to the outward ceremonies of religion, together with a high moral character, I doubt not I shall blot out whatever slurs and stains there have been." Can you suppose that man brought at last to feel that, if ever he gets to heaven, he will have to get there through the righteousness of another? "Through the righteousness of another?" says he, "I don't want to be rewarded for what another man does,—not I. If I go there, I will go there and take my chance; I will go there through what I do myself. Tell me something to do, and I will do it; I will be proud to do it, however humiliating it may be, so that I may at last win the love and esteem of God!" Now, can you conceive such a man as that brought to feel that he can do nothing?—that, good man as he thinks himself, he cannot do anything whatever to merit God's love and favour; and that if he goes to heaven he must go through what Christ did? Just the same as the drunkard must go there through the merits of Christ, so this moral man must enter into life, having nothing about him but Christ's perfect righteousness, and being washed in the blood of Jesus. We say that this is so contrary to human nature, so diametrically opposed to all the instincts of our poor fallen humanity, that nothing but the Spirit of God can ever bring a man to strip himself of all self-righteousness, and of all creature strength, and compel him to rest and lean simply and wholly upon Jesus Christ the Saviour.

These two experiences would be sufficient to prove the necessity of the Holy Spirit to make a man a Christian. But let me now describe a Christian as he is after his conversion. Trouble comes, storms of trouble, and he looks the tempest in the face, and says, "I know that all things work together for my good." His children die, the partner of his bosom is carried to the grave; he says—"The Lord gave and the Lord hath taken away, blessed be the name of the Lord." His farm fails, his crop is blighted; his business prospects are clouded, all seem to go, and he is left in poverty: he says, "Although the fig tree shall not blossom, neither shall fruit be in the vines; the labour of the olive shall fail, and the fields shall yield no meat; the flocks shall be cut off from the fold, and there shall be no herd in the stalls: yet I will rejoice in the Lord, I will joy in the God of my salvation." You see him next laid upon a sick bed himself, and when he is there, he says, "It is good for me that I have been afflicted, for before I was afflicted I went astray, but now have I kept thy Word." You see him approaching at last the dark valley of the shadow of death, and you hear him cry, "Yea, though I walk through the valley of the shadow of death, I will fear no evil; thy rod and thy staff they comfort me, and thou thyself art with me." Now I ask you what makes this man calm in the midst of all these varied trials, and personal troubles, if it be not the Spirit of God? O, ye that doubt the influence of the Spirit, produce the like without him, go ye and die as Christians die, and live as they live, and if you can show the same calm resignation, the same quiet joy, and the same firm belief that adverse things shall nevertheless work together for good, then we may be perhaps at liberty to resign the point, and not till then. The high and noble experience of a Christian in times of trial and suffering, proves that there must be the operation of the Spirit of God.

But look at the Christian, too, in his joyous moments. He is rich. God has given him all his heart's desire on earth. Look at him: he says, "I do not value these things at all, except as they are the gift of God; I sit loose by them all, and notwithstanding this house and home, and all these comforts, 'I am willing to depart and be with Christ, which is far better.' It is true, I want nothing here on earth; but still I feel that to die would be gain to me, even though I left all these." He holds earth loosely; he does not grasp it with a tight hand, but looks upon it all as dust,—a thing which is to pass away. He takes but little pleasure therein, saying,—

"I've no abiding city here,
I seek a city out of sight."

Mark that man; he has plenty of room for pleasures in this

world, but he drinks out of a higher cistern. His pleasure springs from things unseen; his happiest moments are when he can shut all these good things out, and when he can come to God as a poor guilty sinner, and come to Christ and enter into fellowship with him, and rise into nearness of access and confidence, and bold approach to the throne of the heavenly grace. Now, what is it that keeps a man who has all these mercies from setting his heart upon the earth? This is a wonder indeed, that a man who has gold and silver, and flocks and herds, should not make these his god, but that he should still say,—

> "There's nothing round this spacious earth
>   That suits my large desire;
> To boundless joy and solid mirth
>   My nobler thoughts aspire."

These are not my treasure; my treasure is in heaven, and in heaven only. What can do this? No mere moral virtue. No doctrine of the Stoic ever brought a man to such a pass as that. No, it must be the work of the Spirit, and the work of the Spirit alone, that can lead a man to live in heaven, while there is a temptation to him to live on earth. I do not wonder that a poor man looks forward to heaven; he has nothing to look upon on earth. When there is a thorn in the nest, I do not wonder that the lark flies up, for there is no rest for him below. When you are beaten and chafed by trouble, no wonder you say,—

> "Jerusalem! my happy home!
>   Name ever dear to me;
> When shall my labours have an end,
>   In joy, and peace, and thee?"

But the greatest wonder is, if you line the Christian's nest never so softly, if you give him all the mercies of this life, you still cannot keep him from saying,—

> "To Jesus, the crown of my hope,

My soul is in haste to be gone;
Oh bear me, ye cherubim, up,
And waft me away to his throne."

5. And now, last of all, the acts, *the acceptable acts of the Christian's life, cannot be performed without the Spirit*; and hence, again, the necessity for the Spirit of God. The first act of the Christian's life is repentance. Have you ever tried to repent? If so, if you tried without the Spirit of God, you know that to urge a man to repent without the promise of the Spirit to help him, is to urge him to do an impossibility. A rock might as soon weep, and a desert might as soon blossom, as a sinner repent of his own accord. If God should offer heaven to man, simply upon the terms of repentance of sin, heaven would be as impossible as it is by good works; for a man can no more repent of himself, than he can perfectly keep God's law; for repentance involves the very principle of perfect obedience to the law of God. It seems to me that in repentance there is the whole law solidified and condensed; and if a man can repent of himself then there is no need of a Saviour, he may as well go to heaven up the steep sides of Sinai at once.

Faith is the next act in the divine life. Perhaps you think faith very easy; but if you are ever brought to feel the burden of sin you would not find it quite so light a labour. If you are ever brought into deep mire, where there is no standing, it is not so easy to put your feet on a rock, when the rock does not seem to be there. I find faith just the easiest thing in the world when there is nothing to believe; but when I have room and exercise for my faith, then I do not find I have so much strength to accomplish it. Talking one day with a countryman, he used this figure: "In the middle of winter I sometimes think how well I could mow; and in early spring I think, oh! how I would like to reap; I feel just ready for it; but when mowing time comes, and when reaping time comes, I find I have not strength to spare." So when you have no troubles, couldn't you mow them down at once? When you have no work to do, couldn't you do it? But when work and trouble come, you find how difficult it is. Many Christians are like the stag, who talked to itself, and said, "Why should I run away from the dogs? Look what a fine pair of horns I've got, and look what heels I've got too; I might do these hounds some mischief. Why not let me stand and show them what I can do with my antlers? I can keep off any quantity of dogs." No sooner did the dogs bark, than off the stag went. So with us. "Let sin arise," we say, "we will soon rip it up, and destroy it, let trouble come, we will soon get over it;" but when sin and trouble come, we then find what our weakness is. Then we have to cry for the help of the Spirit; and through him we can do all things, though without him we can do nothing at all.

In all the acts of the Christian's life, whether it be the act of consecrating one's self to Christ, or the act of daily prayer, or the act of constant submission, or preaching the gospel, or ministering to the necessities of the poor, or comforting the desponding, in all these the Christian finds his weakness and his powerlessness, unless he is clothed about with the Spirit of God. Why, I have been to see the sick at times, and I have thought how I would like to comfort them; and I could not get a word out that was worth their hearing, or worth my saying; and my soul has been in agony to be the means of comforting the poor sick desponding brother, but I could do nothing, and I came out of the chamber, and half wished I had never been to see a sick person in my life: I had so learned my own folly. So has it been full often in preaching. You get a sermon up, study it, and come and make the greatest mess of it that can possibly be. Then you say, "I wish I had never preached at all." But all this is to show us, that neither in comforting nor in preaching can one do anything right, unless the Spirit work in us to will and to do of his own good pleasure. Everything, moreover, that we do without the Spirit is unacceptable to God; and whatever we do under his influence, however we may despise it, is not despised of God, for he never despises his own work, and the Spirit never can look upon what he works in us with any other view than that of complacency and delight. If the Spirit helps me to groan, then God must accept the groaner. If thou couldst pray the best prayer in the world, without the Spirit, God would have nothing to do with it; but if thy prayer be broken, and lame, and limping, if the Spirit made it, God will look upon it, and say, as he did upon the works of creation, "It is very good;" and he will accept it.

And now let me conclude by asking this question. My hearer, then have you the Spirit of God in you? You have some religion, most of you, I dare say. Well, of what kind is it? Is it a home-made article? Did you make yourself what you are? Then, if so, you are a lost man up to this moment. If, my hearer, you have gone no further than you have walked yourself, you are not on the road to heaven yet, you have got your face turned the wrong way; but if you have received something which neither flesh nor blood could reveal to you, if you have been led to do the very thing which you once hated, and to love that thing which you once despised, and to despise that on which your heart and your pride were once set, then, soul, if this be the Spirit's work, rejoice; for where he hath begun the good work, he will carry it on. And you may know whether it is the Spirit's work by this. Have you been led to Christ, and away from self? Have you been led away from all feelings, from all doings, from all willings, from all prayings, as the ground of your trust and your hope, and have you been brought nakedly to rely upon the finished work of Christ? If so, this is more than human nature ever taught any man; this is a height to which human nature never climbed. The Spirit of God has done that, and he will never leave what he has once begun, but thou shalt go from strength to strength, and thou shalt stand among the blood-washed throng, at last complete in Christ, and accepted in the beloved. But if you have not the Spirit of Christ, you are none of his. May the Spirit lead you to your chamber now to weep, now to repent, and now to look to Christ, and may you now have a divine life implanted, which neither time nor eternity shall be able to destroy. God, hear this prayer, and send us away with a blessing, for Jesus' sake. Amen.

APPENDIX

A Prayer to Live Worthy of the Gospel

"Only let your manner of life be worthy of the gospel of Christ."
Philippians 1:27

~

Most Gracious Heavenly Father,

The word "joy" cannot describe how I feel when I think of how You saved me from darkness and chose me from before time to be adopted into Your family. I praise You for sending Your Son to live a perfect life and die in my place, and for sending Your Spirit to seal, guide, and comfort.

I am grateful for both Your holy love and sanctifying Spirit; and yet I confess my utter imperfection, sinfulness, and need. I have often failed to live a life worthy of the gospel and have treasured sin more than You. I have taken your grace lightly and failed to exalt the Risen Christ with my actions, words, and thoughts. Please help me be ever watchful and prayerful so as to avoid sin. And when I do sin, help me confess it and be quick to repent. O, Lord, rescue me from lies of the world, my flesh, and the devil and reorient my life around Your created reality!

As you speak to me by Your Word, open my eyes to see and treasure Your wondrous truths and understand how they triumph over the world's pervasive (and sometimes persuasive) lies. Cause your Word to shine it's light on my sin, exposing it and making sin disgusting to me. When I read Your written Word, may it lead me to the Incarnate Word—Your Son Jesus Christ. May Your Word by my heart's delight, constant meditation, the default status of my mind; dwelling richly within me.

As I speak to You in prayer, please rid me of distracting or distressing thoughts that drain my prayers' vitality, and cause delight and thankfulness to well up within me to the praise of Your glorious grace. By Your Spirit, draw me nearer to You and guide my intercessions toward greater Kingdom usefulness. May the longing of my heart increasingly be for Your glory displayed in Your image bearers, the building up Your church, and the advance of the gospel around the world.

Thank you for the opportunity and privilege of being a channel of Your grace to others. Fill my lips with Your truth to speak and live out Your gospel to a lost and dying world. Help me follow Christ's example and forgive as I've been forgiven, live with exceeding generosity, bear the burdens of others, encourage the discouraged, show hospitality, and most of all, walk in love. Grant that my fellowship with other believers would nourish and edify like the rejuvenating effects of a rich, soaking rain.

Fix my mind and heart on the glory of Your Son and the sufficiency of His sacrifice. Father, strengthen me to take up my cross and follow Jesus. Help me to boast in only two things: the cross and my weakness that demonstrates Your unmatched strength. Until Christ returns, make me zealous for good works and increasingly transformed into the image of Your Son.

Thank you Father, for the sustaining grace of Your Holy Spirit that makes it possible for me to live a life worthy of the gospel.

—Kevin Halloran (@KP_Halloran). Missionary, blogger, and Bible Teacher. Connect with Kevin at his blog Anchored in Christ (http://kevinhalloran.net).

MINISTRIES WE LOVE

Cross-Points Books loves organizations committed to building Christ's church by proclaiming the gospel, resourcing leaders, and training workers for the harvest. Here are some of our favorite ministries:

9Marks — Building Healthy Churches (www.9marks.org)

Desiring God — Helping people understand and embrace the truth that God is most glorified in us when we are most satisfied in him. (www.desiringgod.org)

Matthias Media — An evangelical publisher of gospel-centered resources. (www.matthiasmedia.com)

Leadership Resources — A global ministry training pastors in 30+ countries to preach expository sermons, train other expositors, and foster movements of God's Word. (www.leadershipresources.org)

The Gospel Coalition — Encouraging and educating Christian leaders by advocating gospel-centered principles and practices that glorify the Savior and do good to those for whom he shed his life's blood. (www.thegospelcoalition.org)

Unlocking the Bible — Delivering the gospel through modern media. The teaching ministry of Colin S. Smith. (www.unlockingthebible.org)